Walking the Old Tracks of the Cheviots

The Archaeology of the Hills

Coquetdale Community Archaeology

First published in the United Kingdom in 2018 by Northern Heritage Services Limited

Northern Heritage Services Limited
Units 7&8 New Kennels, Blagdon Estate, Seaton Burn,
Newcastle upon Tyne NE13 6DB
Telephone: 01670 789 940
www.northern-heritage.co.uk

See our full online catalogue at www.northern-heritage.co.uk

ISBN: 978-0-9957485-6-9

Typeset in Gill Sans

Design and layout by Ian Scott Design

Printed and bound in the UK by Webmart UK

This book has been produced using paper from sustainable
forest sources and environmentally friendly inks

British Library Cataloguing in Publishing Data
A catalogue record for this book is available from the British Library

Maps in this book are based on Ordnance Survey Map Data 1:25 000 scale
© Crown copyright 2018 OS Licence 100056069

Front cover illustration:
The view from the top of Pass Peth

This book was produced with the help of funding from the Heritage Lottery Fund and
Northumberland National Park.

Contents

Preface and Acknowledgements

Coquetdale Community Archaeology (CCA) was founded in 2008 as a spin-off from a community project run by the Northumberland National Park Authority, working mainly in the upper Coquet valley and the surrounding areas.

In 2014, we started researching and documenting the archaeology along the old tracks through the Cheviots. We anticipated that the project would provide opportunities ranging from research to excavation, and would allow us to blend archaeology with local history.

The project has resulted in the publication of two books. The first was *The Old Tracks through the Cheviots*, which examined the history and the archaeology of the Border Roads, the tracks that join what are now England and Scotland. The second is this book; shorter and more portable, it describes a number of walks that visit some of those sites.

We should thank all those members of Coquetdale Community Archaeology – too many to list here – who walked the hills in all weathers and helped plan these routes. And we also thank the Heritage Lottery Fund and the Northumberland National Park, who funded the Border Roads project and without whom none of this would have been possible.

Introduction

There are dozens of walking guides for the Cheviots. Why, you may ask, do we need another?

The difference is that this one focuses on the past as much as the present. In the past, the uplands were busier places, with many more people living there, farming and travelling through them.

The marks of all this are still there. You can walk for just a couple of hours and see things like Bronze Age hut circles, Iron Age camps, Romano-British settlements, medieval field systems and 19th-century whisky stills. The landscape has captured its history – but this is not a history where you need expensive equipment to see what's gone before. All you need to know is where to look. It is an unspoilt landscape.

This guide introduces you to the earthworks, the mounds, the ruins and the patterns in the landscape that you might otherwise just walk past.

The walks in this book are on both sides of the border, ranging from easy outings of a couple of miles or so to ones that are more challenging and will take a whole day. Where possible we have chosen circular routes, rather than ones that send you out into the hills, only for you to have to turn around and come back the same way.

On some of the walks we suggest options that will take you a little further in exchange for seeing an additional interesting site. Where we can, we also point out short cuts and optional return routes that will get you home more quickly if you are pressed for time or if the weather turns against you.

Each walk starts with a short summary that categorises it – Easy, Moderate or Hard – and says how long it is. That's distance rather than time. We don't estimate the latter because different people walk at vastly different rates, and how long the walk will take depends very much on how long you spend browsing around each site. But given the nature of the terrain and what there is to see, it would be an optimistic walker who assumed that he or she could cover more than two miles in an hour. This is a book of slow walks.

We provide logistical information, such as where you can park and a summary of what we think are the highlights of the walk. At the end of the guide there's a glossary that covers the types of ruins and remains you will encounter when out on the hills. To keep this guide portable, these descriptions are brief, but there is much more information in the companion book to this guide – *The Old Tracks through the Cheviots* – which is also published by Northern Heritage. A web site, **www.border-roads.org.uk**, is under development.

When it comes to the walks themselves, wherever possible we distinguish between directions and site descriptions. For the latter we use the same black typeface as this introduction, but when it comes to directions we switch to a colour.

To help the walker we provide OS-based maps for each route; most walks have just one, but one of them uses two. We strongly recommend use of a full Ordnance Survey map as well. The best one is OL16 in the Explorer series, which covers every walk in this book at a scale of 1:25000 (that's 2½ inches to the mile in old money). To accompany this, you will also find a GPS device invaluable and much better than a phone, since reception is very unreliable in the hills. The GPS device will make it easy to use the map references we provide when giving directions and describing locations. We use landmarks and distances as a guide as well, but sometimes there's nothing suitable, and 'turn left at the next sheep' just doesn't work.

We cover other items we suggest you take in the section on Walking Safely.

What you can see on these walks can depend very much on the time of year and the light. The remains of a building that are very obvious in the early spring may be obscured by bracken a few months later; marks of ancient agriculture, like rig and furrow, may be clear with shadows cast by a bright sun, or in frost, but almost invisible on a cloudy day when the light is diffuse.

You should also be aware that some landscape features can change. What is marked on an OS map as an area of forestry may have been felled a few years later, and look completely different.

Finally, for people using satnavs to find the start of each walk, we supply nearby postcodes. However, individual postcodes can cover quite large areas in the Cheviots, and it's advisable to use a map once you are close to your destination.

Walking Safely

There are several things you can do in advance of your walk. The first question you should ask yourself is "am I fit enough?" You should plan a walk within your capabilities and those of any companions. There is no point in planning a 15-mile hike if you only want to walk for around 3 hours.

Ensure that you have an OS map of the area (OL16) and a compass and that you know how to use them. These are particularly important if you are intending to venture off the beaten track. This guide uses a lot of map references; these can obviously be used with a map, but a GPS receiver will be extremely useful.

Then consider the weather. Check local forecasts on the radio, television or on the web and if the weather doesn't look good postpone the walk until it gets better. And remember that the weather can get worse in the Cheviots very quickly, with strong winds blowing in rain, sleet and snow, even in summer.

You should also be properly clothed. A layering system is best but try to avoid cotton in outer clothing (including jeans) because it does not dry well. You also need suitable footwear; make sure new boots have been broken in. Rainproof gear should be carried together with a hat and a pair of gloves. You also need some food and drink. Snacks are best and this is your opportunity to include a couple of chocolate bars. If it is cold you should consider taking a hot drink. Carry all this in a suitable backpack together with some spare clothing and a first aid kit containing plasters, blister pads and any medication you may need.

If you are taking a dog with you, take care to keep it on a lead when near sheep. Avoid cattle completely, because there are instances of walkers with dogs being attacked or charged by cows. If that ever happens, some authorities suggest letting the dog run off, on the grounds that it can outrun the cattle and you can't.

Take a mobile phone but be aware that reception in the hills is unreliable. A whistle is a useful addition, with six short blasts used to summon assistance and three to acknowledge a signal from rescuers. But don't stop blowing if you hear them because they may be using your whistle to track you down.

Before setting out leave details of your route with a reliable person and the time of your expected return together with instructions on what to do if you fail to meet that deadline. Ensure the person is aware of any change to your plans or if you have come off the hills and decided to go visiting. This will prevent any unnecessary call-outs.

However well prepared you are, an incident may still occur. It may not be with your group but with someone you come across. If something does happen consider your own safety first and the safety of the other members of your party before focusing on the casualty. If you are unable to walk the casualty off the hill, assistance is required and you cannot get a mobile phone signal then you will need to send for help. This will involve splitting up your group and whoever goes for help should be fully briefed on the extent of injuries to the casualty, what help is needed and the exact location of the incident. Someone should remain with the casualty and comfort him or her.

You may think we're exaggerating, but it's not unknown for groups to get into trouble on the Cheviots and to have to be helped off the hills by mountain rescue teams and local farmers.

Finally, follow the Countryside Code – protect, respect and enjoy.

•   Look after plants and animals

•   Take litter home

•   Leave gates and property as you find them

•   Keep dogs under close control

Key to Maps and General Information

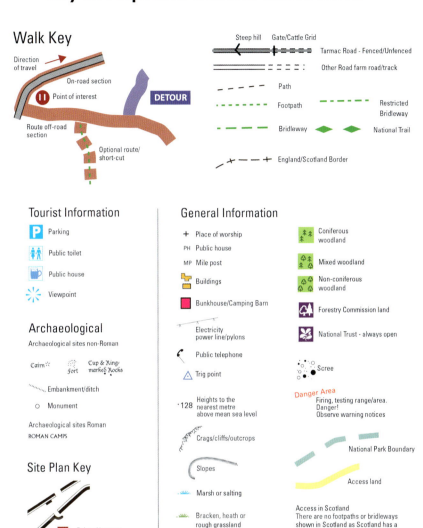

Walk Key

Direction of travel

On-road section

Point of interest

DETOUR

Route off-road section

Optional route/ short-cut

Steep hill   Gate/Cattle Grid

Tarmac Road - Fenced/Unfenced

Other Road farm road/track

Path

Footpath

Restricted Bridleway

Bridleway

National Trail

England/Scotland Border

Tourist Information

P Parking

Public toilet

Public house

Viewpoint

Archaeological

Archaeological sites non-Roman

Cairn

Fort

Cup & Ring marked Rocks

Embankment/ditch

o Monument

Archaeological sites Roman

ROMAN CAMPS

Site Plan Key

F Point of interest (Reference in text)

General Information

+ Place of worship

PH Public house

MP Mile post

Buildings

Bunkhouse/Camping Barn

Electricity power line/pylons

Public telephone

Trig point

·128 Heights to the nearest metre above mean sea level

Crags/cliffs/outcrops

Slopes

Marsh or salting

Bracken, heath or rough grassland

Wall/fence

Coniferous woodland

Mixed woodland

Non-coniferous woodland

Forestry Commission land

National Trust - always open

Scree

Danger Area
Firing, testing range/area. Danger! Observe warning notices

National Park Boundary

Access land

Access in Scotland
There are no footpaths or bridleways shown in Scotland as Scotland has a open access policy

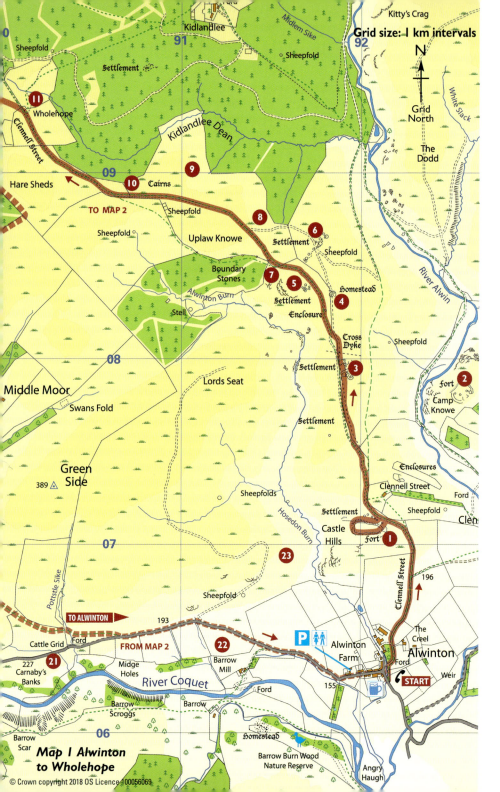

Grid size: 1 km intervals

Kitty's Crag

N

Grid North

Kidlandlee

91

92

Midlam Sike

Sheepfold

Settlement

Sheepfold

White Slack

11

Wholehope

Clennell Street

Kidlandlee Dean

The Dodd

Hare Sheds

09

10

Cairns

9

TO MAP 2

Sheepfold

Sheepfold

Uplaw Knowe

8

Settlement

6

Sheepfold

River Alwin

Boundary Stones

7

5

Homestead

4

Alwinton Burn

Settlement

Enclosure

Cross Dyke

Stell

Sheepfold

08

Settlement

3

Fort

2

Middle Moor

Lords Seat

Camp Knowe

Swans Fold

Settlement

Green Side

389 △

Enclosures

Clennell Street

Sheepfolds

Ford

07

Settlement

Sheepfold

Clen

Hosedon Burn

Settlement

Castle Hills

Fort

1

23

196

Pottsle Sike

Sheepfold

TO ALWINTON

193

Clennell Street

Cattle Grid

Ford

FROM MAP 2

22

P

Alwinton Farm

The Creel

Alwinton

227 Carnaby's Banks

21

Midge Holes

Barrow Mill

Ford

START

Weir

River Coquet

Ford

155

Barrow Scroggs

Barrow

Barrow Scar

Map 1 Alwinton to Wholehope

Homestead

Barrow Burn Wood Nature Reserve

Angry Haugh

© Crown copyright 2018 OS Licence 100056069

Clennell Street, from Alwinton to Wholehope

This walk, starting on Clennell Street, covers archaeological sites ranging from a Bronze Age settlement, through Iron Age remains to remnants of medieval and even 20th century farming. It is always possible to turn back at any stage before the farthest point is reached, which is just over 3 miles from the start, but once there we offer two slightly longer options for a different return.

There are two maps. One (opposite) covers the route between Alwinton and Wholehope. The second, on page 8, shows the two optional return routes. The two maps overlap.

Return direct from Wholehope: 6 miles.
Grading: Moderate.

Via the Wholehope still: 7½ miles
Grading: Hard down to the still and up again, otherwise Moderate, although longer than other walks.

Via Whiteside: 7 miles.
Grading: Moderate; but quite long.

Park in Alwinton (NE65 7BQ) – either where the walk starts on the green on the right as you enter the village from Harbottle or in the National Park car park a little further on round the corner.

Cross the footbridge at NT 9214 0635 on the east side of the green and turn left up the track beyond.

I

After 150 yards this passes Alwinton Farm, and then you start to see the Iron Age camp on Gallow Law ahead and to your left. Clennell Hall is in the valley on your right and after half a mile the track, which has now curved left, is at the foot of the north-east side of Gallow Law.

Turn left towards the Law ❶ when you are 30 yards or so short of the next gate.

Spread over some 90 yards, from NT 9201 0715 in the west (some 70 yards from Clennell Street) to NT 9209 0714 in the east, is a series of at least six hut circles and low banks outlining possible enclosures along the north-east foot of the hill. They are damaged and best seen in winter but are thought to be the remains of an Iron Age or Romano-British settlement.

Follow the path that runs further along the north foot of Gallow Law to the west and then heads uphill.

After 100 yards it passes through a gap in a dyke running along the north side of a plateau below and to the west of the camp.

The camp on Gallow Law from the north. The protective dyke is the thin line on the right ❶

This dyke protected the camp by making access to the plateau harder. Looking west you will see a series of agricultural terraces or lynchets on the far slope. ㉓

Head on upwards but back to the east, through the rocky ramparts and into the camp. Walk across it.

Near the centre at NT 9205 0709 you will find the outline of a rectangular building sheltered by two rock outcrops. Its age is unknown.

Go down the east or north-east side of the hill and back to Clennell Street. Continue up the hill past Clennellstreet farmhouse. 200 yards further on bear right and go though a wooden gate at NT 9204 0747. Continue uphill on the track on the east side of the fence.

After 100 yards or so you will start to get good views of another Iron Age camp – Camp Knowe – half a mile to the east on the other side of the valley. **2**

Continue uphill for another 400 yards.

Camp Knowe from Clennell Street **2**

A scooped Romano-British enclosure ❸

At NT 9189 0790 a low bank appears on the right of the track and parallel with it. This is the first of two; the second, larger one starts 35 yards further on. ❸ These are enclosure dykes that protect two Romano-British settlements. Now damaged, the remains consist of irregular, small enclosures and courtyards – some quite deeply scooped – and about 20 hut circles with diameters ranging from ten to 23 feet.

Just north of this is a good example of a cross dyke, at NT 9187 0803. Up to four feet high, it extends for over 300 yards with its longer section

The Romano-British settlement on the left from the east (Clennell Hill). The rig and furrow is clear and the cross dyke is in the hollow in the centre. ❸
Photo courtesy Matthew Garman

to the east of the path. On both sides of it, and encroaching on the settlement, are stretches of medieval rig and furrow, best seen with a low sun or in snow.

Go through a gate in the fence on your left 100 yards beyond the dyke and continue north along the Clennell Street track 25 yards beyond it to the west.

150 yards further on, at NT 9179 0825 there's a circular low-banked feature immediately to the right of the path. 20 feet across, with a raised centre, this is all that remains of a cairn of unknown date.

Continue for 90 yards past this; the path bears left to the north-west at NT 9178 0834. Stop here and walk five yards east.

50 yards away, on the far side of the fence there is a scooped enclosure about 80 feet across, with a possible house platform inside it and built against the north wall. **4**

Walk on to NT 9171 0841: this is 90 yards past the bend. Stop again and walk south-west up a slight incline for about 40 yards to a plateau. **5**

Here there is a low bank on the far side before the slope continues. This is part of the enclosure of an Iron Age settlement about 40 yards across with eight or nine circular houses, marked by slight grooves up to 18 inches across. Best seen in winter the largest is at NT 9169 0837. Curves in the turf may indicate earlier houses and some rebuilding.

Return to the path.

On the other side of it, about 200 yards away to the north-east, is a sheep stell. To its left, and covering an area 40 yards wide and about 150 yards long (from north-east to south-west), are sets of low banks, enclosures and dwellings. The details are not easily visible from Clennell Street, but there are five enclosures in all, representing the remains of yet another Romano-British settlement. **6**

Continue north-west. After 200 yards you approach a gate in a dip.

This is an area of disturbed ground, with several dykes, ditches and banks. **7** One of these may be a cross dyke and is most prominent to the south-west of the path at around NT 9147 0844. In the same area (NT 9150 0841) is a segment of another ditch that consists of multiple holes that have not been joined up. It's been suggested that this is of military origin, the holes being dug by individual soldiers before the project was abandoned.

Carry on to the north-west. About 300 yards past the gate, at NT 9134 0869, turn back on a path that comes in behind you on the right. Follow this for 75 yards and then turn north (left) for 15 yards. **8**

You are on the edge of a small enclosure centred on NT 9141 0872. This is egg-shaped, 45 yards long (north to south) and 35 yards wide. It contains two substantial hut circles, the larger of which is 40 feet across. Originally, this was almost certainly a small Iron Age palisaded settlement.

Go back to Clennell Street and continue north-west for about 250 or 300 yards.

Sheep pens are visible about 200 yards further on, and the same distance away to your north (right) you will see lines on the moors, several of which are approximately at right angles to each other. **9** Best seen from a distance, these low banks are the remains of a Bronze Age field system and the associated dwellings. One of these roundhouses has been excavated and was found to be some 4000 years old.

Continue on Clennell Street, which is now heading west.

Before reaching the next gate, the track passes between two ruined cairns, each about ten feet across, at NT 9077 0890 and NT 9081 0888; it then cuts through a low bank and ditch of unknown origin at NT 9071 0888. **10** Near the fence is a circular structure some 12 feet across with some large stones clustered on the eastern side. It's been claimed that this was a pit for cockfights, but if so it's very small and in a very unusual style; it's more likely to be the remains of a hut or a small house.

Carry on for three-quarters of a mile up a gentle hill from the gate; the path arrives at what's left of Wholehope Farm. **11**

The main surviving feature is a low ruined wall, but until 1942 this was a substantial working farm. There is rig and furrow in the field to the east of the farm, and a stock enclosure that was probably linked with it about 150 yards to the south-west at NT 9002 0922. The building was used as a youth hostel in the 1950s but was finally abandoned in 1964.

The ruins of Wholehope 🔴11

At this point, you can either go back the way you came, or else select one of two possible return routes that pass different sites. These are shown on the map overleaf.

Wholehope when a working farm 🔴11

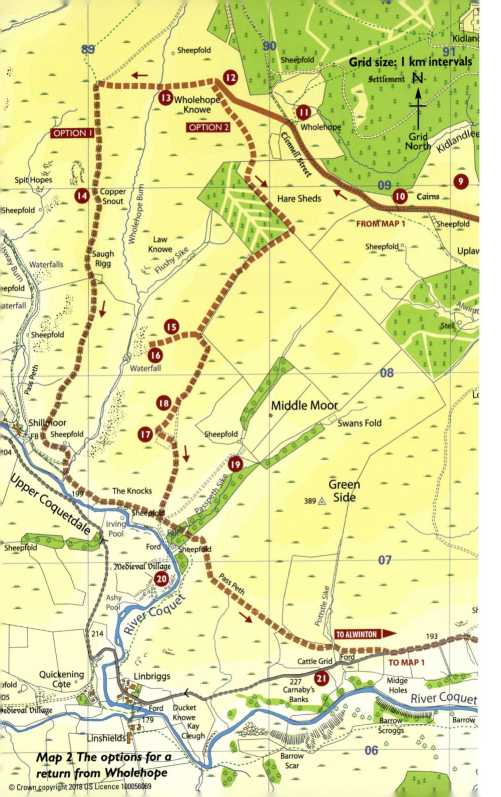

Grid size: 1 km intervals

Settlement N

Grid North

89

90

91

Kidland

Sheepfold

Sheepfold

Kidlandlee

12

13 Wholehope Knowe

OPTION 1

OPTION 2

11 Wholehope

Clennell Street

Spit Hopes

14 Copper Snout

Sheepfold

Hare Sheds

09

10 Cairns

9

FROM MAP 1

Sheepfold

Wholehope Burn

Law Knowe

Flushy Sike

Sheepfold

Uplaw

Saugh Rigg

Waterfalls

sway Burn

epfold

aterfall

Alwint

Sheepfold

Pass Peth

15

16 Waterfall

Stell

08

18

Middle Moor

Shillmoor

FB

Sheepfold

17

Sheepfold

Swans Fold

The Knocks

199

19

Green Side

04

Sheepfold

Passpeth Sike

389

Upper Coquetdale

Irving Pool

Ford

Sheepfold

07

Sheepfold

Medieval Village

20

Pass Peth

Ashy Pool

River Coquet

Pottsle Sike

214

TO ALWINTON

193

Sh

Quickening Cote

Linbriggs

Cattle Grid

Ford

TO MAP 1

epfold

05

Ford

179

Ducket Knowe Kay Cleugh

227 Carnaby's Banks

21

Midge Holes

River Coquet

edieval Village

Linshields

Barrow Scroggs

Barrow

Barrow Scar

06

Map 2 The options for a return from Wholehope

© Crown copyright 2018 OS Licence 100056069

One of the quarries on Wholehope Knowe ⑫

For either of these routes, go through the gate just past the farm ruin, then leave the track and head north-west to the top of Wholehope Knowe at NT 8969 0957. Sometimes there is a path, but the going is not hard.

There are pits and hollows at the top, which are almost certainly the remains of old quarries. ⑫

You can now head west to the remains of the Wholehope whisky still, go south down Copper Snout on the far side of the Wholehope burn to Shillmoor and then return to Alwinton. Or, you can head roughly south from the top of Wholehope Knowe and visit the remains of what was probably a medieval settlement at Whiteside ⑱ before joining the Alwinton path about half a mile south-east of Shillmoor. This is slightly shorter and easier.

Option 1: Return via Wholehope Still

The remains of several illegal whisky stills have been found in the Cheviots, but only one has been excavated – that near Wholehope which was investigated by John Philipson in the early 1950s. He showed it probably dated from the late 18th and early 19th centuries.

The still is only 300 yards to the west from the top of Wholehope Knowe, but there is no good path to it and access involves a very steep descent, dropping some 300 feet to the burn.

Head towards NT 8944 0948, where on the steepening slope you may pick up a narrow track that heads straight down the hillside to a point about 25 yards downstream from the still. The still itself is at NT 8940 0953 on the east bank of the Wholehope burn and opposite a small bay in the hillside on the west. **⓭** However, do not head straight for it from the top of the Knowe as this will lead you over a sheer 20 foot drop above the ruins.

Working upstream, the first structure consists of the remains of the kiln. This is circular and built into the slope; attached to it, on the burn side, is a small rectangular building that was presumably used to store fuel and as a place from where the kiln could be stoked. Next to this, and moving upstream, is a larger rectangular building and then a two-roomed building of a similar size. Depending on the time of year, these may be very overgrown.

This must have been a very difficult site to excavate. Parts of it are very wet, and access was not easy. It is thought that the first of the two larger buildings was used to malt barley, because it has a cobbled floor, while the one upstream may have been used for living and working, perhaps housing the still itself.

Cross the narrow burn and head west up the flank of Copper Snout towards NT 8904 0955. There is no path, but the slope is not as steep

The kiln at the still **⓭**

as the one you came down, and the worst bits can easily be avoided. Near the top is a track at around NT 890 095. Turn south (left) on this.

After about 750 yards, the route cuts through a cross dyke at NT 8904 0886. ⑭ Immediately south of this there are the remains of two shielings, one on either side of the path. If these are contemporary with the dyke it's not known what they were for, but they may have been built later, perhaps using the dyke as shelter.

One of the shielings by the cross dyke on Copper Snout. The dyke runs off to the lower right ⑭

Continue downhill. As the track nears the farm at Shillmoor it briefly turns east and then back to the south. At the next corner, where it turns west, drop down a path to the south to a gate and pick up another path that runs parallel with the river.

At NT 8941 0722 this meets a farm track. Head to NT 8956 0719 to pick up the other return route that went past Whiteside and crosses the Passpeth Sike (page 14).

Option 2: Return via Whiteside

From the high point on Wholehope Knowe at NT 8960 0943 you will see a broadly rectangular area to the south that was once forested but now has trees re-growing on it.

Head south-east to NT 8978 0939 to avoid the wettest of the intervening ground and then south and downhill to a crossing point on a fence at NT 8988 0913. Then cut across the rough ground to the north-east fenced edge of the once-planted area, bear left and follow it to its eastern tip.

Here you turn right (south-west), through one gate to a second; this is in a fence at NT 8988 0860, beyond the southern tip of the once-forested area. Go through this and follow the track that ends up running parallel to the fence some 40 yards to the west of it. Follow this south-west for 500 yards to a point near another gate at NT 8963 0821. Then head west and slightly downhill for just over 150 yards to NT 8947 0819. **⑮**

Here there is a roughly square enclosure with edges about 50 feet long. Hollows and stones on its western side hint at some form of building inside it. 25 yards to the south is the start of a ditch or sike heading west.

Follow this downhill for about 100 yards to NT 8937 0818. **⑯**

On the south side of the sike are the remains of a rectangular dwelling or shieling about 60 feet long and 20 wide; there are suggestions of an interior wall two-thirds of the way along from the sike. The structure is deep in bracken in the summer but is in a spectacular position on a terrace overlooking the drop to the Wholehope Burn. On the north side of the sike is another square enclosure at NT 8940 0822. This is slightly larger than the one uphill but is also often covered in bracken. These are no dates for any of these structures, but it's possible they are contemporary with the settlement you're about to see back on the main path and further south.

Go back uphill to the path by the fence and continue south. After about 150 yards, as the track cuts over an old dyke, ahead and to the right you will see a square stone stock enclosure some 500 yards away. **⑰** This is the next destination but there are objects of interest before it.

As you drop down a slope you will see traces of rig and furrow draped over the saddle that lies between you and the stone enclosure. Once you leave the main slope, about 40 yards west of the track is a dwelling or shieling at NT 8943 0782. **⑱** It is 45 feet long with a clear interior wall a third of the way along it.

The first shieling you'll come to at Whiteside 18

About 40 yards to the north at NT 8943 0786 is a similar structure but this is deep in bracken in summer. There are the remains of a third building to the east of the main track at NT 8952 0784.

Head directly towards the stone enclosure from the first structure.

The rig and furrow you cross can be faint (see picture on next page) but a low dyke on the right clearly acts as a field boundary. Just to the north-west and south-west of the enclosure you will see the ghostly outlines of its predecessors. The 'modern' one has been built on top of – but offset from – an earlier one, and there are the remains of that in the form of the footings of an old stone wall inside the later structure. There has also been activity about 25 yards south-west of the enclosure; large hollows mark old quarries, but one of them may have been repurposed as an enclosure. 40 yards further south-west, at NT 8932 0763, are the faint remains of two more dwellings or shielings, near the end of a dyke that drops down the slope to the north-west.

All these structures may well be the remains of the settlement known as Whiteside, first referred to in medieval documents and shown on 17th century maps. It wasn't the only settlement in the area. Another straddles the Passpeth Sike down in the valley 500 yards to the south-east; centred on NT 8942 0754 are the remains of four buildings and some associated enclosures. 19

Rig and furrow across the Whiteside saddle

Follow the old low stone wall from the north-east corner of the 'modern' enclosure back to the track.

You pass a circular structure 20 feet across at NT 8946 0767. This may be an old stack stand but it's small; it clearly predates the wall which has been built over it.

Take the track south for about 500 yards. Along this stretch you can see the route you are aiming for, Pass Peth, ahead and to your left as it runs up the western slopes of Green Side. The track broadens out and at NT 8953 0729 you cross a farm track.

Continue south-east, join the other return route and cross the Passpeth Sike at NT 8956 0719. Ignoring turnings to the right continue on the main path up the hill.

As you climb, pause to look at the remains of the medieval village of Linbrig ahead and down to your right, lying on the far side of the river between an improved field and a point where the Coquet flows close to the hillside. **20** The walk does not include a detour to visit this site because fording the river can be difficult.

Follow the path over the corner of Green Side; it then starts to drop back into the Coquet valley.

About 350 yards past the highest point there are old field systems below on the right, cut through by the road. **21**

The view west from the top of Pass Peth

Head diagonally downhill aiming for a gate by a sike at NT 9036 0655. 300 yards beyond this you reach the road through another gate at NT 9066 0651, about a mile from Alwinton.

After about half a mile along this road, you pass a track on the right that runs down to Barrow Mill. **22** (on the first map). This was a corn mill on the Coquet, which was first recorded in 1712 and had ceased operation by 1860. There are still the remains of a corn drying kiln on the site and the leats that managed the water flow to and from the mill can be seen from the road. The building is now a holiday cottage.

Arrive at Alwinton and the car park.

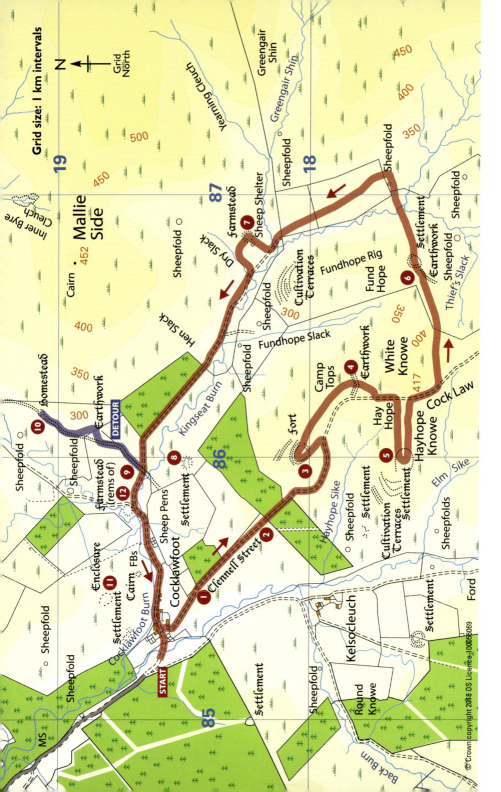

Clennell Street, south from Cocklawfoot

This is a circular walk north of the border that takes in a number of Iron Age sites – such as camps, farms and homesteads – as well as some later activity. The climbs are not arduous, and while there is one short stretch without a path, this is downhill and not too difficult. Towards the end of the walk there's an optional detour of about 600 yards uphill (and the same coming back).

Distance: About 5 miles.

Grading: Moderate.

Drive south on the road along the Bowmont valley that leaves the B6401 at Primsidemill. Park on the west bank of Bowmont Water at around NT 8521 1858, just short of Cocklawfoot farm (TD5 8QA).

Cross the bridge towards the farm and go through the farm gate. After some 50 yards turn up a track on the near side of the first farmyard building on the right. This is Clennell Street.

The dyke above Cocklawfoot just before it turns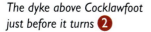

As you climb, the path starts to run parallel with a bank or dyke, cutting through it on occasions. This is one of the many boundary dykes in the area. Just before you pass the first forested area on your left stop at NT 8551 1844 . ❶ Look back at the farm, the area around it and the valley of the Kelsocleugh Burn to the west. Banks, old field boundaries and enclosures are all remnants of ancient farming activity.

Carry on to NT 8577 1816, just before you enter another forested area.

The large dyke ❷ that was parallel with the path curves round and heads downhill. Once through the trees, the Iron Age camp at Hayhope Knowe ❺ is visible straight ahead, and if the light is right you may see traces of cord rig on the hillside below it.

Hayhope Knowe from Clennell Street, seen from south of Camp Tops ❺

Continue for about 400 yards to NT 8617 1789, where the track curves right and levels off slightly. Take a path to your left and behind you to another Iron Age camp – Camp Tops. ❸

On the top of the hill and in the shape of a D, the camp measures about 200 feet from east to west and 150 feet north to south. No large ramparts can be seen as you approach from the south-east, but there are impressive ones elsewhere, especially to the north where there is a triple rampart with a ditch up to ten feet deep. The earthwork 40 yards downhill from here is an old hollow way, marking an earlier route of Clennell Street (far right in picture below).

The camp has entrances to both east and west; the latter is slightly sunken and cuts through a section of rampart where some stonework is visible. The roundhouses inside are not always easy to see, but there is a good example on one of highest points at NT 8603 1804, and others extend in a line to the west.

The northern ramparts of Camp Tops **3**

Leave the camp and head south-east along the ridge, over a low hillock to NT 8626 1781. Here a short cross dyke spans the ridge.**4** Once past this bear half right and re-join Clennell Street; continue south for about 150 yards to NT 8621 1759 and turn right down the track to the camp on Hayhope Knowe.**5**

The structure measures about 350 feet from east to west and 200 feet north to south. The path enters the camp through a single rampart that was probably built to protect a settlement that was initially in a weak defensive position. The rampart is incomplete; its best sections are to the north and east, leaving the other sides protected by steep slopes. The settlement it defended originally had a double palisade around it that is now inside the rampart. This is very hard to see, but a section is just visible as two parallel grooves some six feet apart at NT 86013 17609 about 50 feet west from the top of the eastern rampart. All the huts were behind this palisade, and their remains consist of various scoops and platforms. These are generally clearer on the west side of the camp; a large one is at NT 85990 17626, and a second at NT 85959 17610.

Return to Clennell Street and continue south and east for 200 yards to NT 8630 1745. Take a faint track on the left which soon becomes clearer as it heads east. After 200 yards you will see two gates: one of them, on the right at NT 8648 1749, is in a fence that runs from approximately east to west. Go though this and as you follow the track downhill along the south side of the fence you will see the marks of an enclosure on the south end of Fundhope Rig straight ahead. ❻

The green outline of the settlement on Fundhope Rig ❻

As you drop into the intervening valley of Fundhope Slack there is a dyke on the right at NT 8671 1755, which was probably built to control stock movements into or out of the valley. The settlement on the Rig that was visible earlier is centred on NT 8675 1759, ahead and up the hill. It measures about 140 feet from north to south and 120 feet from east to west, and was once encircled by a palisade. The remains of this are practically invisible on the east side but are best seen on the north-west around NT 8673 1761 where the bank that supported it is about nine feet across with grass of a slightly different colour. There is an entrance here as well at NT 8674 1761; extra ramparts outside this may have provided additional protection from an approach along the ridge. Inside, scoops and hollows hint at huts, the best one being about ten yards south of the entrance at NT 8674 1760.

Head down the steep hill from the east side of the settlement; there is no path, but aim for the sheep stell on the far side of the valley. Cross the Kingsseat Burn at the foot of the slope; this is not hard but there is an old footbridge just downstream from a point opposite the stell. Aim for the gate at NT 8701 1766; go through this to the stell, and then head roughly north along the wide grass track just beyond it. After about 600 yards and just past a bridge at NT 8682 1815, turn right up a track to a circular enclosure at NT 8684 1823. **7**

This is about 130 feet across and is surrounded by a low stony bank over a foot high in places; there's an entrance to the east. On the south side is a modern shed next to an older stone sheep fold. The shed is in a sunken area; this may be the site of an earlier building, perhaps one contemporary with the fold, and aerial photographs show signs of cultivation elsewhere in the enclosure. A low bank runs past the west side of the enclosure, and there are some ten small rectangular buildings along its length as it heads north towards the watercourse of Dry Slack. Many of these are eroded or hidden by bracken but an obvious one, about 20 feet long and nine wide, is in a grassy area at NT 8678 1826. The original enclosure is probably Iron Age in date but it seems that the location was re-used in medieval or post-medieval times for a small farmhouse and a set of shielings.

The enclosure at Dry Slack **7**

Go back to the track and continue for about half a mile, past a forested area to NT 8607 1865.

Across the burn to the south-west, about 200 yards up the slope and on the near side of a dry stone wall is an area of disturbed ground and a couple of banks. **8** These are the remains of a Romano-British settlement.

Continue round a bend to the west for another 120 yards to NT 8596 1866. Here, the path cuts through a dyke whose ditch on the burn side has been dug out for drainage. **9** You can either continue on the path or, if time and energy permit, detour from it briefly to see the next site. If you do this, head uphill through the gate and follow the dyke for about 500 yards. You pass various field boundaries and (with a slight detour to the right to use another gate) arrive at a homestead at NT 8616 1905. **10**

The scooped homestead or settlement on the dyke **10**

Of unknown date, this consists of a deep scoop in the hillside, roughly circular and about 75 feet across. The bank surrounding it has some stonework visible in places; it is not high but the scoop into the hillside is such that parts of the interior are over ten feet deep. An entrance on the south-west leads into this often bracken-filled interior; on the east side a stone-reinforced terrace holds the remains of a dwelling. The relationship of the scoop and the long dyke it straddles is such that it's not easy to work out which is older, but other factors suggest that the homestead is prehistoric, while the dyke marks a medieval boundary, perhaps linked to the farmstead in the valley that is the next destination.

The old farmhouse east of Cocklawfoot ⓬

Return down the dyke.

About halfway down look to your right and roughly west; about half a mile away you can see a pattern of dykes and an enclosure on the shoulder of the hill on the far side of the Cheviot Burn in the valley below you. ⓫ These are probably the remains of a medieval or early post-medieval farmstead.

Once back on the track continue west towards Cocklawfoot.

After 200 yards a track comes in from the right, running down the east side of the Cheviot Burn. About 20 yards up the track, and to its west in a meander of the burn, is a bank forming an irregular enclosure measuring about 120 feet from north to south. The track has cut through its east side, turning it into a D-shape, while about 60 feet to the east of the track is another bank forming part of another enclosure about twice the size.

On the south side of the D, at NT 8578 1869, are the remains of what was probably a medieval farmhouse, whose western end has been partly washed away by the burn. ⓬ What's left is a rectangular ruin about 40 feet long; there are no real signs of internal divisions, but some stonework can be seen in the external walls. These are badly eroded in places, making it hard to be sure where the original entrance was.

Continue to Cocklawfoot, passing yet more old banks and enclosures near the farm.

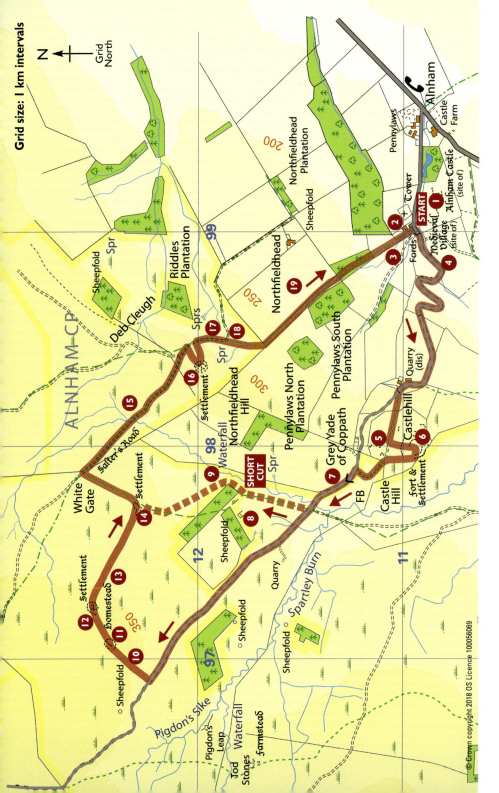

Alnham and The Salter's Road

This walk starts and finishes with the medieval, but in between it visits an Iron Age camp with Romano-British additions, two of the finest Bronze Age palisaded settlements in the area and then more Iron Age settlements and a ruined farm. This is a circular walk based around Alnham, with its second half on the Salter's Road. A short cut avoids high ground. Otherwise, there is a long but mostly gentle uphill section along an unfrequented metalled road, and one downhill section where there is really no path, although the direction is clear.

Distance: About 5 miles: the short cut reduces this by a mile.

Grading: Moderate.

Park on the verge by Alnham church at NT 9911 1093 (NE66 4TL).

The core of the church dates from the 12th century, but there are later additions; Saxon masonry blocks in the nave hint at an earlier building.

Part of old Alnham village ❶

The field on the other side of the road from the church contains the remains of part of the old village, abandoned some 300 years ago. ❶ 'Alnham Castle', an old pele tower, is the mound on the skyline to the left of the picture on the previous page, while lower down and just slightly to the right is another enclosure which contains a house platform. There is rig and furrow at the top, and banks below this and on the right are old field boundaries. The main part of the village, however, was in the field to the east of the church, and cannot now be seen.

Follow the road west for 100 yards to a large house next to the church. This is the Vicar's Pele. ❷

Originally a 14th century tower, it fell into disrepair but was restored in the early 19th century, and the adjoining house was added. The battlements date from this period. Now a private house, it was a youth hostel from 1944 to 1958. Just past this and the footpath north, the road runs next to a drystone wall. On the slope above it is an extensive set of hollow ways. ❸ These mark the tracks taken by centuries of traffic to and from the moors beyond; this was the most direct way in and out of the village and from the roads beyond without trampling over the village fields to the east.

About 50 yards past the cattle grid, there is rig and furrow coming down the hill to the south. ❹ This is another of the old village fields – Castle Field.

Old tracks to the moor ❸

The south-west rampart of the camp on Castle Hill **6**

Follow the metalled road uphill through some zig zags. Depending on the light, as you look back you may see more old rig and furrow. After three-quarters of a mile you pass Castle Farm. 50 yards further on, just before a cattle grid, a finger post on the left marks a track going uphill though a gate at NT 9824 1102. Follow this, go through a second gate and follow a low bank on your right – the footings of an old field wall – until you reach a bank across the path.

This is one side of a roughly rectangular enclosure **5**, with the remains of a roundhouse towards its far side at NT 9807 1105.

Turn left towards a larger bank on the near skyline.

This is the outer rampart of the Castle Hill Iron Age camp. **6** Cross it to another enclosure built over the inner ramparts and a second roundhouse at NT 9801 1098. Like the other enclosures along the north-east and east sides of the camp, these are Romano-British and so are later additions to the site.

Cross the ramparts – three in all – and walk to the centre of the camp at NT 9799 1094.

There are no obvious house remains in the interior, so the camp was probably never densely populated. There are high ramparts to your left overlooking the valley to the south-east and the open country beyond.

Turn right and head in the direction of the hilltop cairn on the far skyline, towards another prominent rampart that is higher than the surrounding sections.

This overlooks a steep drop 100 yards beyond and faces up the valley to the north-west. With natural protection already in place, were these distinctive ramparts built for show rather than defence?

Pick up a track heading north from the north end of this section of rampart and go to a gate in a drystone wall just over 100 yards away at NT 9791 1108. Continue north-west to another gate at NT 9786 1115; go through this and drop down to the road at around NT 9788 1123. Turn left.

The Grey Yade of Coppath is the large stone on your right after some 50 yards at NT 9785 1126. ❼ The Coppath Burn is just down the hill, and Yade is a dialect term for a horse – usually one past its best. It is possible to sit on the stone.

Walk down the road to the burn; 40 yards past the bridge there's a finger post on the right saying 'White Gate'.

The Grey Yade of Coppath ❼

Short Cut

Turn here to make use of a short cut on the walk; the actual path leaves the road on a diagonal some ten yards past the post at NT 9769 1146, and then runs roughly north, parallel with the burn.

Also visible from the road, there are old enclosures uphill to the left of the short cut at NT 9767 1178. **8** Low walls and banks on the slope mark old field boundaries that may be medieval and the outline of a farmhouse was once visible near the track above the enclosures at NT 9766 1181.

Enclosures from an old farmstead **8**

Continue on the short cut, reaching a gate at NT 9783 1186.

There are hollow ways running across the path just beyond the gate. **9** These lead down to the burn at NT 9786 1187 and are the remains of an old road from Alnham that can be traced further up the valley.

Turn half left up the hill after the gate on a faint and badly damaged path. Avoiding the sedge on the right, you will soon pick up guideposts on the path that leads to your destination – the settlement at NT 9770 1229 **14**, where the short cut ends. Pick up the route on page 31.

Main Route

Continue uphill from the Coppath Burn; the road crosses another cattle grid at NT 9725 1193. Three-quarters of a mile from the burn take a path to the right, at right angles to the road, at NT 9685 1227. If you reach a point where the road turns left quite sharply you've gone about 100 yards too far.

Before leaving the road look back to the camp on Castle Hill and see the prominent rampart facing up the valley.

Follow the path uphill onto High Knowes for 120 yards. At NT 9698 1235 you cross a low bank. ⑩

This is the south-western stretch of a dyke nearly two miles long that encircles the entire hill at the 1200-foot contour, forming a roughly oval enclosure of some 120 acres. In some places, especially to the north-west of the hill, it's indistinct, but elsewhere it is nearly two feet high.

Continue uphill for another 120 yards onto the shoulder of the hill, where there are two structures that may well be connected with this dyke.

At NT 9706 1241 you come to the south-west edge of a circular, double-palisaded settlement some 50 yards across. ⑪ This is believed to date from the late Bronze Age, and so is over 2500 years old. The shallow trenches marking the palisades are eight to ten feet apart, and despite its age the low mound between them still has shorter and greener grass. There are only four roundhouses in this first settlement,

The marks of a double palisade ⑪

30

the most obvious one being some 15 yards from the palisade and centred on NT 9706 1243. Crossing the settlement, you pass the entrance through the palisade on the east side at NT 9709 1242.

Follow the high ground across the shoulder of the hill; 140 yards and roughly north-east of the first settlement you come to a second one at NT 9720 1248. **⑫**

Here the palisade, although clear, is less well-defined. Depending on the vegetation you can make out over a dozen roundhouses, the best one being in the south-east quadrant at NT 9724 1250.

Leave the eastern side of the second settlement at NT 9727 1251 on a narrow track that heads south-east and downhill. After 200 yards, at around NT 9739 1236, re-cross the dyke encircling the hill. **⑬** Now head slightly left (east-south-east), ignoring any tracks to the right and continue downhill; the path may get faint and lost in a wet area with growths of sedge.

By now, however, you should be able to see your destination – a grassy area at NT 9770 1229, just up the slope from a path that runs past it on its eastern side. This grassy area is home to an Iron Age or Romano-British settlement. **⑭**

The main route joins the short cut here.

The settlement is in the shape of a rough oval aligned approximately north-south and divided across the centre by a bank about 100 feet long. On its eastern side, next to the path, are adjacent entrances to each of the two resulting yards. Various ridges and banks inside hint at structures, but two roundhouses are among the most obvious. One is on the south side of the bank separating the two yards at NT 9772 1229. It's quite small at 15 feet across, but a larger one, about twice the size, is 50 feet up the slope at NT 9770 1230. A possible third is further south at NT 9771 1227 and there may be others.

Pick up the path running along the east side of the settlement and head north for 300 yards to the White Gate at NT 9788 1255. This is where the Salter's Road comes up from Alnham on its way to Ewartly Shank and the border. Go through the gate and head south-east along the Salter's Road to re-cross the Coppath Burn at NT 9811 1232.

A hollow way near the Coppath Burn **15**

There are obvious hollow ways both here and a bit further on at NT 9825 1218. **15**

Continue for about 400 yards south-east beyond the burn. At NT 9842 1208 the path meets a broad farm track just by a guidepost; now turn right (south-west) uphill for 80 yards. A faint path takes you to an Iron Age settlement centred on NT 9837 1198. **16**

The remains are very indistinct. Aerial photographs show a low bank forming a circular enclosure with about 15 roundhouses inside; the best of these is at NT 9838 1200, just up the slope from a large clump of sedge. The site has a great view over the valley, as does a similar settlement on Hart Law, about half a mile to the north-east.

Return to the track by the way you came and follow it south to NT 9850 1189, which is about 20 yards short of a bend to the left.

Here, a substantial bank on your left heads north-north-east. **17** Probably medieval, this was a head dyke, which protected the cultivated land below it from stock grazing on the moorland above. With the ditch always on the uphill side, it also controlled water draining off the moor. This dyke is quite long, running mainly east for about a mile, and if the light is right you can see rig and furrow and banks marking old fields between the dyke and the modern fields below.

Continue down the track to the bend and then bear right towards piles and lines of stones at NT 9850 1183. **18**

This is the ruin of the old Northfieldhead farm (one with the same name was built later further downhill). You can still make out the remains of two adjacent and overlapping rooms or compartments. One of these may have been a byre, and if you look closely at some of the lines of stone, you can see old masonry blocks partly hidden by the rubble. The farm was last mentioned in parish records in 1771, and the fields around it were abandoned around that time.

The ruins of Northfieldhead farm 18

Walk down the slope towards the fence past other banks and enclosures, one of which may contain the remains of another stone structure. Turn right along the fence and go to the second gate which is at NT 9847 1166. Follow the track downhill for 1000 yards to the south-east.

The North Field of the old Alnham village is on your left but it is now all under modern cultivation. 19 At NT 9888 1113, as you enter the field above the Vicar's Pele, you come to the hollow ways you saw at the start of the walk 3; some are on the far side of the wall on your right, while others are nearer the path. Looking to the south, you may see the rig and furrow in the old Castle Field on the far slope. 4

The path brings you out on the road 100 yards west of the church.

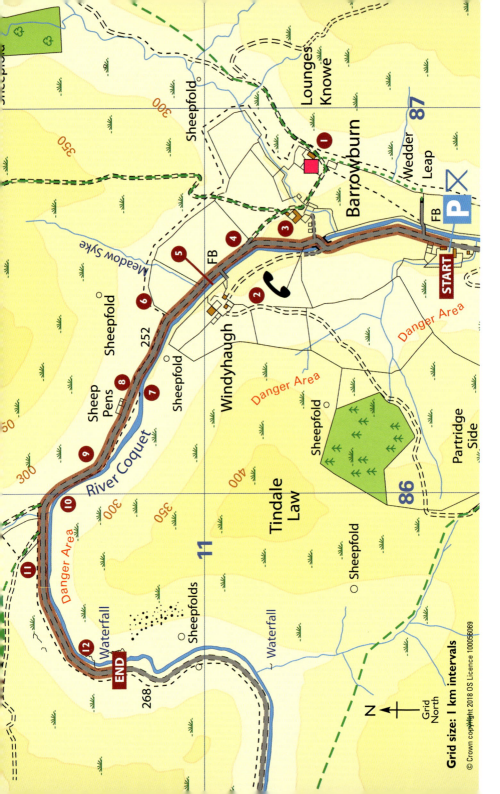

Lounges Knowe

Sheepfold

Sheepfold

Barrowburn

Wedder Leap

87

1

P

3

4

5

FB

Meadow Syke

2

FB

START

Danger Area

6

252

Windyhaugh

Sheepfold

Sheepfold

Danger Area

Sheepfold

8

Sheep Pens

7

Partridge Side

9

River Coquet

300

350

Danger Area

Tindale Law

400

86

10

300

350

11

Sheepfolds

Waterfall

11

Waterfall

Sheepfold

300

Danger Area

Waterfall

12

END

268

Sheepfolds

N
Grid North

Grid size: 1 km intervals

© Crown copyright 2018 OS Licence 100056069

Barrowburn:
A short walk along The Street
The upper reaches of the Coquet

A walk along a little-used metalled road. There are no significant hills, and you can retrace your steps at any time. This is a short stretch of a road, The Street, that dates back to medieval times and beyond. Near the end of the walk at Slymefoot, the old track climbs into the Cheviots, crosses into Scotland and connects with routes to Kirk Yetholm and Hownam.

The walk passes through the remains of a once-busy agricultural landscape. The medieval monks of Newminster Abbey owned this land and left evidence of their activity behind them. This includes the remains of a mill, which **CCA** excavated between 2011 and 2014.

To reach the start of the walk take the single-track road up the Coquet valley from Alwinton for about 5 miles.

Distance: About 2½ miles   Grading: Easy

Park at the Wedder Leap car park at NT 866 103 (near NE65 7BP). As you leave the car park, turn left and pass a brown building.

This was once called Askew Hall, and was a social centre for the surrounding area and beyond with dances, bands and even radio broadcasts. It is now used as a barn, but still has a dance floor inside.

Passing the footbridge on your right the modern Barrowburn farmhouse ahead of you becomes increasingly obvious; to its right, up

The old school

the slope and under some trees about 300 yards away, you will see a stone barn and a wooden bungalow with a green roof.❶

The barn is what's left of a farm called Lounges Knowe. Now used for camping, it acted as a school from around 1880, and the bungalow next door was built for the schoolmaster. In 1971 the site closed and a new school was built where the car park is now. But this had a short life, closing in 1978 and then being demolished. As you continue up the road you may see rig and furrow in the field above Barrowburn.

Go past the turning to the farm on your right and the one to Windyhaugh on your left.

Both farms are over 300 years old and Windyhaugh may be medieval. Up the hill to your left is a single large ash tree. ❷ This may be the survivor of the 'three venerable ash tees' under which the Presbyterian ministers of Harbottle once

The preaching tree ❷

The old Barrowburn farm circa 1930 with a long peat stack to its right. ❸ *Windyhaugh is in the distance and the ruin of Lounges Knowe is on the right.* Photo courtesy Bill Trobe

preached, attracting congregations from far afield. On your right, behind the modern Barrowburn farm, is the old slate-roofed farmhouse.❸

Continue to a point where the road swings left and a farm track joins it from the right. ❹

Until the 1930s, the road up the valley used to go past the far side of the old Barrowburn farmhouse and then turn left (see picture above). The track is where it crossed the fields and joined the current road.

Walk for another 100 yards to a flat area on your left by the river bank with a telegraph pole on it. About 20 yards upstream from two concrete abutments that once supported a footbridge are the remains of a medieval mill that was used for fulling, a process that removes grease from newly woven cloth and tightens it up. ❺

Tucked in under the near bank is a line of moss covered blocks that were once part of the wheel pit. In the 13th century the land here was owned by the monks from Newminster, near Morpeth. As part of their wool business, they built this mill between 1226 and 1244, but it was probably abandoned less than 100 years later. The pit held a wheel about 11 feet across, and just downstream was a wooden platform in the river that

The mill's wheel pit 5

was probably used for washing cloth. More details can be found in *The Old Tracks through the Cheviots*, this guide's companion book.

Follow the road for another 250 yards; 45 yards past a drystone wall on the right and at a crest in the road, a substantial ditch and an earthen bank come down the hill on the right. 6

This was a medieval boundary marker built by the monks, who as well as the mill had a farm or grange in the Rowhope valley a little further on. The dyke runs over the top of Barrow Law, which is the hill on your right, and may have joined up with similar structures on Middle Hill further east.

The boundary dyke 6

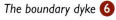

Look across the river to see a good example of a stone sheep stell.

These acted as shelters where a shepherd could manage sick stock or pen them for lambing and marking.

The longhouse from the other side of the river **7**

70 yards further on, also on the other bank, are earthworks forming a rectangle about 70 feet long and 20 wide with openings at the downstream end and the far side. **7** This may be the remains of a longhouse, one part of which was lived in with the other part used for stock. Excavation of similar remains behind Barrowburn farm dated them to the 17th century, but they were on top of a medieval structure with a well-built stone flagged floor.

The longhouse from above the road on Barrow Law; one entrance is at top right **7**

Look to the right of the road when opposite the downstream end of this structure; you will see a low bank running away from you. **8**

This turns upstream after 20 yards, where it forms a low shelf in the hillside. It then follows a line almost parallel with the road until reaching the trees behind the modern sheep pens 100 yards further on. This bank defines the edge of a large stock enclosure; further along, it emerges from the trees 25 yards from the road and runs parallel with it for 70 yards before turning down to the river. **9**   In all it encloses an area of about 1.5 acres. This clearly dates from a time when there were more sheep in the area, and perhaps stock brought along The Street from Scotland by drovers.

Continue for another 150 yards.

Best seen by scrambling up the hill a bit, there's an old rectangular enclosure on the far bank of the river about 40 yards short of the point where the road forks. **10**   One branch of the fork goes to the farm at Rowhope while the other crosses the bridge over the Rowhope Burn just before it joins the Coquet.

Field boundaries by the Rowhope Burn. The enclosure is in shadow just left of the bottom centre and The Street runs parallel with the bank across the left of the picture **11**

To the north-west, the line of The Street climbs the hill on the far side of the Rowhope Burn. **11**   On its right is a bank that defines an old field and within that, down by the burn and opposite the right hand end of the triangle where cars park, is the outline of a small rectangular

Traces of old cultivation

enclosure. This may be linked to an old farm here called Slymefoot, which was apparently also a drinking house for the local community. Its reputation was such that in the middle of the 18th century the rector of Rothbury ordered it to close.

Cross the bridge and walk up the road above the river. Watch out for any traffic here; getting off the road is not easy. About 400 yards past the bridge and opposite the second (longer) stretch of wooden fencing, you will see a flat area on the far bank about 25 yards wide and 70 yards long.

If the grass is short you will see that this area is bounded by shallow ditches and low banks running down to the river at each end. The first of these is opposite a low waterfall in the river and the second is opposite the upstream end of the fencing. The land between them covers about a third of an acre and consists of narrow lazy beds, sets of low ditches and banks that were used to grow vegetables and crops. Of unknown date, earthworks just to the right of the upstream boundary bank may be the remains of a house or shieling.

This is where the walk ends, so retrace your steps to the car park.

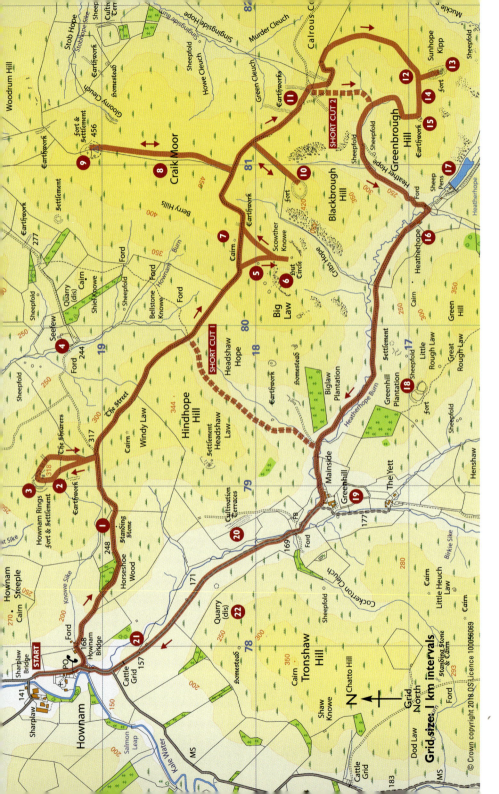

The Street from Hownam towards the Border

This is a walk along **The Street** from Hownam, in the old Scottish county of Roxburghshire. Heading south, it takes in sites ranging from Iron Age camps and farms to houses and structures that were only abandoned in the 19th and 20th centuries.

Potentially long, you can easily make the walk shorter.

The initial part of the walk is along **The Street**, south from Hownam. At any stage you can retrace your steps.

Most site visits involve detours from **The Street**. Any of these can be left out.

A short cut helps you return before the final two sites.

One person can return to Hownam early and drive south to meet fellow-walkers near Mainside Farm on the return leg.

Distance: 11 miles for the full walk
Grading: Hard, but short cuts can make it moderate

Park at Hownam (postcode TD5 8AL). This may be difficult in the main street without blocking a house but there are places at the north end of village near the bridge where you can park off the road. Walk south through the village.

150 years ago the first house on the right was the village school and Post Office. Further on, in the 19th century two of the houses used to be inns. The first, just before the old telephone box was the Shepherd's Arms, while the next house (The Old Coach House) was the Dickson's Arms.

Leave the road at the south end of the village at NT 7786 1914. Here the road curves to the right; take a track to the left that turns and leads uphill. Follow this track through two gates and past Horseshoe Wood on your left.

The interior of the original horseshoe shape has been filled in by later planting, but old curved walls in the wood show its original shape.

There are quarries in the fields on your right, as well as rig and furrow; once past the wood the track runs across this and it's on both sides of you. Look across the valley to the right to see agricultural terraces on the flank of Tronshaw Hill. **22**

150 yards after the wood is a single standing stone some 35 yards south of the track at NT 7874 1890. **1** It may have been re-erected at some stage and the adjacent large hollow might be the result of an early excavation.

Continue on the track which leads up a slope alongside a wall. 550 yards after passing the stone you reach NT 7920 1904. Go through the gate by the fingerpost.

A low bank or dyke on your left heads north. This may have once marked a boundary between two estates; the track ahead is an old route that connects Hownam with Belford in the Bowmont Valley.

The standing stone near Horseshoe Wood **1**

Leave The Street and follow a faint path crossing more rig and furrow and running along the east (right) side of the dyke, which becomes more prominent. After 140 yards the dyke turns north-east and the path heads north-west for just under 200 yards to NT 7907 1928.

You are at the western end of a line of stones 120 yards long called the Shearers. ❷ There are 28 in all, but some are small and lying deep in the grass. They are probably the stone core of a now-vanished bank or earthwork, although there is a local myth that they are the remains of reapers that worked on the Sabbath.

Continue north-west for about 100 yards, past a small rocky mound on your right: you will now be next to the ramparts of the Iron Age camp of Hownam Rings at around NT 7901 1935. ❸

The ramparts go all around the camp but are most prominent on the west where four are very clear. In places they are four or five feet high and 30 feet across. The site was excavated by Margaret Piggott in 1948; she concluded that the camp had been built in multiple phases, starting with a settlement with a single palisade in the 1st or 2nd century BC. Now believed to be several hundred years earlier, this has all but disappeared, but was followed by the construction of increasingly robust defences.

The Shearers, looking west ❷

The north side of Hownam Rings. ❸ *The area with the houses is to the right of the ramparts*

Climb to the top of the steep slope of the southern ramparts, turn left and walk clockwise around the camp.

The multiple western ramparts are on your left: at NT 7901 1941 the defences start to drop down a slope and the outer ramparts become less striking. 90 yards after climbing the ramparts, and stretching away to the east for some 30 to 40 yards, is a relatively sheltered area with scoops and platforms which are the sites of ancient roundhouses.

These are not the only ones on the site, but Piggott thought that these were built late in the camp's life. Excavation of one of them unearthed thick stone walls and Roman pot sherds from the late 3rd century AD, suggesting that Hownam Rings was in use for over 700 years.

One of the scooped house sites

To the north is the imposing bulk of Hownam Law. On its southern flanks is the abandoned farm of South Cote. First recorded in 1621, it was still in use in the 20th century.

Walk across the area with the house sites to the eastern edge of the camp just over 100 yards away.

Here, mostly outside the ramparts and centred on NT 7912 1938, are the remains of a homestead that Piggott also thought was built late in the camp's life. It consists of low banks forming a rectangular enclosure 70 or 80 feet across with dwellings inside it. The most obvious sign of one of these is a platform measuring about 25 feet by 20 near the northern side of the enclosure.

Head south-east for 200 yards from the homestead past the eastern end of the Shearers.

The abandoned farmhouse of Seefew **4**

You cross a large area of rig and furrow. Aerial photographs show substantial expanses of this all around the camp, and the area was obviously once heavily cultivated, probably as early as the medieval period.

Turn right once you meet the dyke you saw earlier and follow it to the point where you left The Street. Turn left and continue east and then south-east along the track beside the wall, keeping it on your right.

You will see a ruined farmhouse in the valley below you on your left. **4** This is Seefew, next to the old road from Hownam to Belford, and it was abandoned in the 1880s. The track drops and passes through a gate at NT 7992 1844.

Short Cut 1

40 yards after this gate a track leads off to the right. You can either use this to cut the walk short or as a later option if returning along The Street. It leads south-west along the side of Headshaw Law and after three-quarters of a mile joins the return route in the valley at NT 7924 1758, about 300 yards east of Mainside Farm (page 60).

Main Route

Continue on the track, with the fence on your left, for nearly 600 yards to NT 8031 1810, a point where the fence turns slightly left at the top of an incline. Don't follow the track by the fence but continue uphill for 30 yards and then bear half right along a narrow path heading just east of south for some 150 yards to NT 8040 1797.

You are at the eastern side of one of a line of three circular structures. ⑤ Another is 120 yards to the west at NT 8026 1792 and the third 40 yards beyond that at NT 8021 1790. Each is bounded by low banks and they have diameters of between 35 and 55 feet; none of them has an obviously original entrance. They are not dateable, but are almost certainly stack stands which stored fodder for local cattle or those being driven along The Street.

Continue for about 70 yards along the path to a small pointed mound at NT 8045 1792.

The ground drops away from you and then rises again. On the far slope you can see narrow bands that mark the presence of cord rig.

Cord rig at Scowther Knowe ⑥

This is essentially hand-built rig and furrow and is typical of Iron Age farming. The site is called Scowther Knowe and the fields are near the 1200-foot contour, so growing conditions were not ideal. **6**

Walk downhill and up the far slope to NT 8043 1775.

Just below the top of the slope is a shallow circular ditch marking the site of a roundhouse about 35 feet across, with faint remains of a smaller one beyond it. Aerial photographs show a surrounding circular enclosure some 100 feet across, and the people that lived here probably cultivated the adjacent fields. The site is exposed and on the edge of a steep drop down to the valley, but has unbeatable views.

Little Rough Law. The main camp is in front of the trees, with the annex to the right **18**

Look across the valley to the south-west. About three-quarters of a mile away, just to the left of a large plantation, is the Iron Age camp of Little Rough Law. **18** The main part is in the centre of the picture; it's oval-shaped, about 200 feet long with a stone-faced rampart built round the edge of the hillside. There's a similar-sized annexe on a saddle to the north-west (right).

Return to the small pointed mound and then turn half right, roughly north-east, towards the fence line about 250 yards away. The map reference you are aiming for is NT 8063 1808.

As you walk, you will see a substantial cairn on your left on the far side of the fence. **7** The prominent pile of stones is modern, but it has been built on a very much older structure about 40 feet across.

The cairn, with modern additions **7**

You reach The Street by the fence as it climbs a short, steep slope, taking the form of an interwoven set of hollow ways. About halfway up, and on the fence side of the path, are the remains of a dyke that may once have stretched right across the route.

Turn right and follow the path as it turns north and then east again (you can cut the corner). 400 yards after the first turn you come to two gates on your left at NT 8096 1815. Go through the smaller of these and head north across Craik Moor on a path that runs to the east (right) of the fence.

You pass two small standing stones on your right and then a third just as the fence changes direction slightly. Beyond this there are six more, some on the other side of the fence. **8**

One of the standing stones on Craik Moor **8**

Not quite in a straight line, they are separated by distances of between 60 and 140 yards. Some are up to two feet high, but they have no visible markings, and it's not known what they were for.

Continue for just over half a mile from The Street until you see an old trig point on the fence line ahead of you.

Here you see an obvious sign of defence. At NT 8110 1899, 40 yards short of the trig point, is a pair of shallow ditches curving away to the north-east. These mark the site of a double palisade that once stretched across the neck of land at the north end of Craik Moor.

Then, just two or three yards short of the trig point, are the remains of a low earthen bank studded with stones. In the right conditions signs of other single palisades to the south of the trig point can be seen as well. All these defences were clearly built to defend a settlement beyond them.

The most visible remains of this are two roundhouses. One is seven or eight yards past the trig point and three yards east of the fence; its ditch or gully shows it was about 27 feet across. The other, slightly larger, is just on the other side of the fence.

The double palisade trench at the north end of Craik Moor

Stonework in the Craik Moor defences **9**

Go through the gate in the fence.

On your right are the substantial remains of a stone wall; there is a lot of loose tumble, but a line of dressed stones can be seen within it. **9**

At almost 1500 feet, the camp or fort this protected is the highest in the Cheviots, and it must have been built as a defence against incursion from the moor. Fragments of low banks can be made out at a few places around the rest of the promontory, but much material has obviously been used to build the drystone wall that bisects the structure, and a modern sunken and embanked path on the east side has done further damage.

One of the house sites beyond the stone defences

There are the remains of several house sites beyond the wall, but the two most obvious are the two closest to it, about five and ten yards respectively away from the stone tumble.

This is a complex site. A plausible sequence of events starts with Late Bronze Age or Early Iron Age dwellings protected by one or more banks and palisades, with the presence of people on the site culminating with the substantial stone defences near the north end of the spur which protected newer houses beyond it.

The outturn across the ditch at the entrance to Blackbrough camp ⑩

Retrace your steps to The Street, turn left and continue south-east for 250 yards to a gate at NT 8114 1801. Take a track to the right ten yards after the gate; walk for 400 yards across a narrow ridge to the entrance to Blackbrough camp at NT 8089 1775. ⑩

On reaching the camp you'll see that the ends of the impressive inner ramparts on either side are turned out at right angles, blocking access to the ditch outside them and making the entrance a narrow corridor roughly ten feet wide and 50 feet long. The sides of these defences have a few boulders embedded in them which may be the remains of a more solid structure, but otherwise the ramparts consist largely of earth and rubble.

The inside of the camp is almost empty. The one visible feature, and even this is not obvious, is a shallow trench forming an oval around the centre of the camp, about 110 feet long and 80 feet across.

The Blackbrough ramparts

This is best seen if you follow the path across the camp from the entrance. After 65 yards, at NT 80849 17704, there is a shallow groove on either side of the path, but best seen to the right as it runs away to the north-east. It may have once held a palisade, perhaps forming an enclosure that either predated the camp or else protected the people who were building the ramparts.

Return to The Street and continue south-east for just under 400 yards, coming down a slope to NT 8133 1774.

The Street passes through a gap some 50 yards wide in the first of three cross dykes. ⓘⓘ A second dyke is about 160 yards further on at the foot of the slope at NT 8142 1760, and the gap in it is much narrower. Both dykes are nearly 400 yards long, and each consists of a single bank and ditch.

The palisade trench inside the camp

Walk through the second cross dyke. Several different tracks fork off here at NT 8142 1760 or just beyond. One heads east through a gate, while another goes straight up the slope in front of you. Do not take either of these. The walk's main route is slightly to the right and climbs the slope ahead more gently by skirting round it to the south, passing the southern end of a third dyke on your left at NT 8151 1753.

Looking south along the ditch above the second of the three cross dykes

Sets of triple dykes are rare but not unknown. There are two more in the area – one on Raeshaw Fell to the south-west and another some two miles to the south on Callaw Moor. As with other cross dykes, their original function is unknown although they probably formed some sort of defendable boundary. But it's unclear why three would be built so close together.

Short Cut 2

If you want to cut the walk short by just over a mile, take the option of a fourth track some 40 yards after the second cross dyke. This is to the right of the main path and sets off downhill from NT 8145 1757. After 40 yards (NT 8145 1754) you reach a fork; take the left hand path and go south down a steep track along the floor of a wide gully. 300 yards further on this swings right and south-west. After another 150 yards, at NT 8136 1722. a path comes in from the left (south). This is the track from the final sites, and you re-join the main route here (page 59).

Main Route

Follow the track identified before the short cut. After passing the third cross dyke it climbs round to the left and then right in a hollow way and up to a fence. Walk along this for 50 yards; as the path levels off at NT 8171 1755 a fainter track bears off diagonally to the right and south-east. Follow this for 400 yards to a grassy area at the top of a gentle rise. At NT 8185 1719 bear slightly right, walking along a path to the south-west, parallel with a fence and about 20 or 30 yards from it. After roughly 400 yards you reach NT 8157 1692.

At this point the path passes between two circular structures that are almost certainly stack stands. ⓬ The one on your left is about 40 feet across and the one on your right about 50 feet. There is a third, more ruined one, on the same line about 70 yards away to the right; this is slightly larger again. These stack stands reflect agricultural practices that were much later than the structure that's about 50 yards away – downhill and on your left. This is the rampart system of the defended settlement of Sundhope Kipp. ⓭

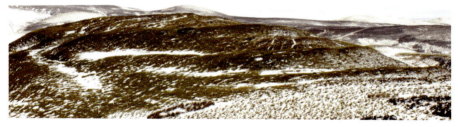

The Sundhope Kipp ramparts. ⓭ *The entrance is the curved path on the left*

Walk south down the slope and cross the settlement's ramparts.

There are four of them and they would have been built as a defence against attack along the ridge from the north. There is no direct entrance through them and access to the settlement is on its east side in a hollow way shaped like a reverse S. This too would have been defendable. The defences around the sides other than the north take the form of very steep slopes, so the whole site was fairly secure. In contrast with the empty interior of Blackbrough, Sundhope Kipp seems to have been densely populated, with the area beyond the ramparts

Hut grooves in the Sundhope Kipp settlement

covered in closely packed hut circles. There are over 20 of them; some of them are fragmentary and some overlap – built on top of earlier ones – so the site was clearly used for several generations.

Look just west of south from the southern end of the settlement. On the other side of the valley of the Heatherhope Burn below you are the remains of a large circular enclosure. Damaged in places, it's nearly 200 feet across; on the uphill side of the interior are two platforms that may once have held dwellings.

Return to the track running between the two stack stands, turn left and head due west through a gate for 300 yards onto the western end of Greenbrough Hill.

The circular enclosure (on the right) across the valley from Sundhope Kipp. The hillside is covered in tracks and boundary lines old and new

As you cross the intervening saddle, you are walking through another area of cord rig, marking agriculture that may date from the same period as the settlements here.  **14** This is high up (1250 feet), very faint, and best seen from Sundhope Kipp itself.

At the western end of the hill there are two slightly higher areas. On the first, at NT 8132 1692, is another type of settlement. **15** A shallow trench in the shape of a rectangle about 90 feet by 70 once held a palisade. A break in the trench on the north-east side marks an entrance and inside there are the remains of two roundhouses – one in the centre about 25 feet across (NT 8130 1691) and another, slightly smaller and fainter, in the southern corner.

Cord rig on Greenbrough Hill **14**

The eastern corner of the palisade trench on Greenbrough Hill **15**

Rig and furrow and old fields above Heatherhope

Head north and downhill from here. There is no path but after 170 yards you meet a track running across the hillside at NT 8130 1708. Turn right and follow it as it curves left and down a steep slope to a T-junction at NT 8136 1722. This is where you'd be if you followed the short cut downhill from the three cross dykes. Turn left and downhill along a valley called Heather Hope.

After just over half a mile you come to the main Heatherhope Burn; on your approach you can see marks of old rig and furrow and field boundaries on the hillside opposite. There is a bridge over the burn at NT 8074 1688 by a farm building, which 19th-century maps show was the old Heatherhope farmhouse.

Snow melt run-off from the Heatherhope reservoir

Cross the bridge over the burn and turn right on the farm track that runs along the valley floor.

About 200 yards upstream from the bridge is the part-dismantled dam of the Heatherhope reservoir. **17** Built to supply Kelso with water, further down the valley are squat iron posts marked KWW – probably Kelso Water Works.

Walk roughly north-west down the valley. This track, which becomes a road after Mainside Farm, leads back to Hownam. It's about 2½ miles.

After about half a mile, at around NT 8000 1724, the two hummocks of the top of Little Rough Law are above you on the left, but the ramparts of the camp you saw from Scowther Knowe are hard to see from below. **18**

As you approach Mainside Farm you will see another, larger building behind it on the left. This is Greenhill Lodge. **19** Built in the early 19th century as a shooting lodge for the Duke of Roxburghe, it had a different use in the 1940s when it housed evacuated pupils from the Steiner School in Edinburgh.

About 250 yards past the farm, there is a substantial area of agricultural terracing in the field on your right, and more of this can be seen above the modern fields about 400 yards further on. **20**

70 yards beyond the remains of a pillared gateway at NT 7870 1774, the road passes by the remains of an old homestead. Banks on the left-hand verge may be due to road construction, but a rectangular outline can be seen over the fence in the field above you at NT 7866 1780.

Agricultural terraces near Mainside farm **20**

The hollow way down to the Heatherhope Burn **21**

Continue for about three-quarters of a mile to a small brick building on your right at NT 7800 1870. **21**

There are banks on either side of it. Those about 40 yards to the north extend beyond the nearby stone wall and form a deep hollow way down to the burn.

Look over the wall directly behind the building and you will see a faint platform on the far bank of the burn about 60 yards away.

Part of the possible site of Kirkraw Mill **21**

These structures may be the remains of Kirkraw Mill, marked on maps some 200 years ago.

Walk for another 500 yards into Hownam and to your car.

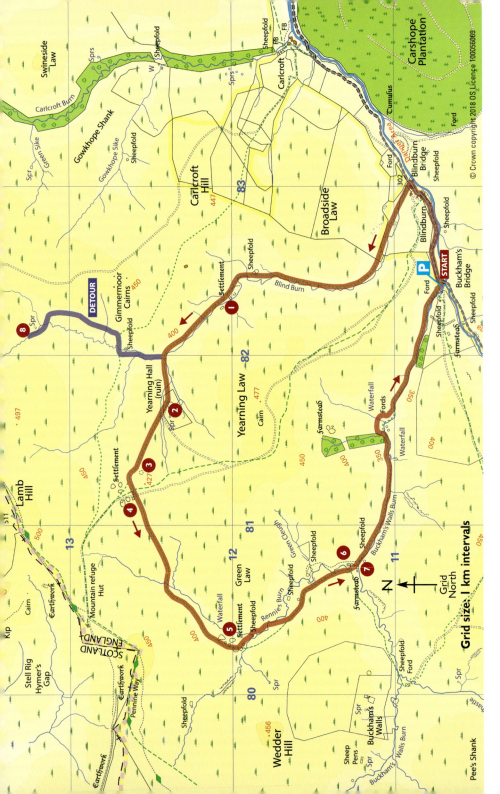

The Blind Burn, Yearning Hall and beyond

This route connects with the next walk which goes along the Buckham's Walls Burn. It too passes through an area of old farms and settlements, some of which may have been medieval in origin; one was operating until the mid-20th century.

The walk goes up the Blind Burn, passes traces of settlements and reaches the remains of Yearning Hall farm. Now almost destroyed, it was lived in until the 1940s. A detour takes you further up the burn to an abandoned whisky still, while the main path visits a substantial set of ancient stock enclosures and shielings near the border. Then there are more medieval or post-medieval shielings before reaching the ruined farm on the Rennie's Burn. Here you join the Buckham's Walls Burn walk and return to the start.

Distance: 5 miles, with the whisky still detour adding 1½ miles

Grading: Moderate
(although a summer detour to the whisky still can be hard)

Park at the Buckham's Walls Burn car park at NT 8241 1071, about 600 yards west of Blindburn farm (NE65 7DD). Walk to the farm and follow the signed footpath through the gate on the left just beyond the farmhouse. Follow the Blind Burn upstream.

60 yards after crossing a bridge a rectangular enclosure bounded by low banks at NT 8278 1098 marks the remains of an old stock enclosure.

The settlement on the Blind Burn (centre left) and circular enclosure (right, below shed) 🔴

Continue for another three-quarters of a mile to a ruined sheep stell on a patch of raised ground. Cross a boggy area where the track can be hard to make out. About 200 yards past the stell there's an area of dryer grassland which starts at NT 8241 1199.

On the left, 70 yards further on at NT 8234 1202, are the remains of a two-roomed building close to the burn. 🔴 With substantial walls still in place (but covered in turf), this was probably a dwelling with an attached byre, although there are no historical records for it. Next to it on the downstream side are banks surrounding an irregular enclosure and there's a separate circular one 30 yards downstream. When the vegetation is low you can also make out a low dyke that starts near the path just past the upstream side of the building at NT 8235 1202, runs down the east side of the grassed area at the foot of the slope, and goes past the shed before turning down to the burn, making an enclosure of just under an acre.

Another 70 yards upstream and on the far bank at NT 8229 1206 are more ruins. You can see these from the path, but if you scramble across the burn, you will find a narrow rectangular building about 50 feet long and ten wide, which appears to have been divided into two or even three sections. Just downstream is a roughly rectangular area cut into the slope. About 25 feet square, it might have once held a building, or been made for some activity that needed a level surface.

Yearning Hall today ②

Walk 600 yards further upstream on the main path and cross the burn at NT 8198 1239, where a small stream joins it from the west. Follow the track that runs above the north bank of this tributary.

200 yards to the west, up a sharp incline, are the remains of Yearning Hall farm at NT 8176 1239. ② First recorded in 1777 it was lived in until at least 1940, with a baby being born there that April. The building lies roughly east-west, and is divided in two. The western section was the byre, while the dwelling house was to the east. There were windows on both sides of this section, and the front door was in the middle of the south side. The dwelling area was in turn divided into two parts, with what was probably a bedroom in the south-east corner, with the fireplace. Most of the rest was a living room and kitchen, with a range against the wall between it and the byre.

The picture on the next page shows what the farm used to look like. The smoke from the central chimney is from the range, a house cow grazes on the left, and a garden is at lower right.

From Yearning Hall you can either continue the circular walk or make an out-and-back detour to the Blind Burn whisky still. The detour is described at the end of this walk.

If continuing, leave the fenced area around the farm by the gate on the north side, go through a wet area and follow a track from NT 8164 1245 west and slightly north towards a guide post on the near skyline. Cross a grassed area to around NT 8135 1259, where an ellipse of paler grass can be seen on the left. Leave the track to reach it at NT 8131 1256.

This is an old stack stand ❸, but it is unusual in that it has a very prominent ditch around it. Built to store and protect fodder, this one is about 50 feet across. The spoil from the ditch has been used to build a low bank around the outside and slightly raise the interior, perhaps to help with drainage.

Yearning Hall probably circa 1930. Photo courtesy Bill Trobe ❸

Return to the path and continue along it. You will now see low dykes ahead that define an enclosure. Pause after some 200 yards at NT 8120 1266 (**A** on the Lamb Hill site plan opposite).

In summer it may be harder to see but you are now approaching a complex set of shielings and enclosures. ❹ There is no particular recommended sequence in which to tour them, but items to look for include a shieling at NT 8112 1270 (**B**), and a rectangular enclosure just to the south of it at NT 8112 1267. (**C**) Just north of the shieling at NT 8113 1271 is the start of a curved bank (**D**) that can be traced to at least NT 8116 1269 and which may have been longer. East of this are

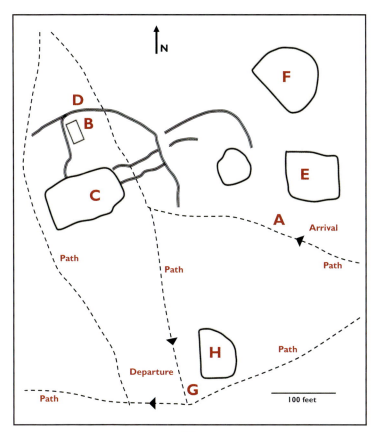

The main enclosures on Lamb Hill. ④ *Be aware that on the ground the site is more complex*

more dykes and ditches, and at NT 8124 1268 is the rectangular enclosure you first saw (**E**). North of this at NT 8122 1273 is a D-shaped enclosure (**F**) with a wall on the south-west side that is still between two and three feet high. You will find other dykes and ill-defined enclosures as well.

The complexity of the site suggests many phases of use, but we don't know who the users were. It may have been part of some English shieling grounds listed in the area in 1604, but there were earlier reports of Scots bringing stock south for the summer, and the site is only half a mile from the current border.

Go south to a guide post at NT 8118 1258 (**G**) next to another enclosure (**H**) and follow the path west. The next destination is ahead

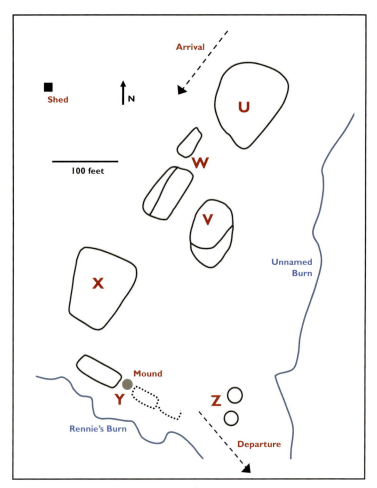

The settlement by the Rennie's Burn ⑤

and to the left – a grassed area below the skyline with a dark shed on it. The path turns south-west after 250 yards or so, and about half a mile further on reaches the junction of two burns at NT 8064 1236. Cross the one coming down from the north (the right) and follow a faint path on the far bank approximately south-west, keeping the burn on your left and about 20 or 30 yards below you. After a quarter of a mile you arrive at the raised grassy area: the highest point is the shed at NT 8025 1206.

There are several enclosures and dwellings here ⑤, between the burn you have been following and the Rennie's Burn that joins it from the north-west.

*Part of the settlement by the Rennie's Burn (**V**)*

To the east of the shed is a D-shaped enclosure at NT 8034 1205 (**U** on the plan), an irregularly-shaped one south of it at NT 8033 1200 at the top of a steep slope (**V**) and then two sub-rectangular structures back to the west, the larger centred on NT 8030 1201 (**W**). It's not entirely clear what these latter two are, but they may be some combination of a steading with a byre and a yard.

Heading south-west from these, you come to a larger enclosure centred on NT 8026 1197. (**X**) The bank surrounding it is clearest at the top; on the steep slope down to the Rennie's Burn, it's been suggested that this made it unsuitable for stock but better for crops, especially as it is south-facing. Below this and a little to the east is a long narrow terrace above the burn where there are the remains of three steadings or shielings in a line (from east to west: NT 8034 1194, NT 8030 1193 and NT 8027 1194). (**Y**) The first two are faint, but the third, just west of a small hillock or mound, is almost 60 feet long and may actually be two abutting buildings. This terrace was probably a good place to live or work, being close to water and having some shelter. Further east on the terrace are two overgrown circular structures. (**Z**) Only some 12 feet across, they're too small to be houses, and were probably built for some undefined agricultural activity.

Head south-east down the Rennie's Burn. There are several paths along the valley floor, but no single one seems to go the whole way. If you take this route you may sometimes have to cross the burn but this is usually easy. The path marked on the OS map stays a little to the west, and runs along the higher ground there. It's hard to find where this leaves the Rennie's Burn, and one way back is to start by heading to the stone sheep stell at the junction of the two burns.

The stell is later than the settlement but footings of old walls, particularly just to the south of it, suggest that there was an earlier, larger structure here. Just downstream from the junction of the two burns there are stone outcrops on the west bank at NT 8038 1178; these may be an old quarry.

Cross the burns near their junction and head downstream along the east bank of the Rennie's Burn. After 250 yards you come to a small area of haugh land with some stone outcrops on your left. Just beyond this, at NT 8050 1166, cross the burn, climb the small hillock ahead and walk along the ridge parallel with the burn for about 70 yards. A path is now visible on the other side of the sike in front of you, below you and slightly to your left. This is probably the footpath on the OS map. It can be clearly seen for a little way, but although it then gets fainter it can still be followed along the hillside for about 350 yards to NT 8074 1127.

Look below you to your left. On the far side of the burn are the remains of two small buildings. **6**

The remains of two buildings near the junction of the Rennie's Burn with Buckham's Walls Burn **6**

The ruined farmhouse by Buckham's Walls Burn 7

Their purpose is unknown, but they may well have been connected with the ruined farmhouse at the junction of the Rennie's Burn and the Buckham's Walls Burn some 50 yards on. 7 Just downstream from the junction is a large oval enclosure with a more recent sheep stell inside.

Here you join the path of the next walk (Walk 7), which gets you back to the car park along the north bank of the Buckham's Walls Burn. There used to be a bridge over the Rennie's Burn by the farmhouse, but now the best place to cross is at NT 8076 1127, a ford by the two small buildings described above.

The oval enclosure just below the Rennie's Burn junction

The walk down the valley of the Buckham's Walls Burn is just over a mile, and follows the first part of the next walk in reverse. For a longer outing follow that walk to Buckham's Walls farm (page 79) and then back over Eald Rigg. This is about three miles.

Detour to the Blind Burn Still

When the main path up the Blind Burn gets close to Yearning Hall, rather than cross the burn at NT 8198 1239, stay on its eastern bank and follow a track north; this fades away after 200 yards. Cross the burn and an area of haugh land, probably by staying close to the fence on your left.

Past a ruined stell, a track comes in from the west through a gate in the fence. You now have two options. You need to get to NT 8220 1315, a fork at the head of the main valley some 500 yards to the north. In winter the valley floor is passable, but otherwise bracken and long grass make the going very difficult, and there is no path all the way. But there is an alternative.

Climb the track to the east (up a couple of hollow ways) for some 150 yards to about NT 8212 1270 and then strike north along the valley side.

As you approach the fork on this route drop down to the valley floor and follow the bank of the burn to NT 8219 1311 where you cross it. Take a path north-west up the left hand side of the fork. In winter stay close to the burn but in summer go higher to avoid nettles.

The ruined still consists of low turf-covered walls forming a rectangle about 18 feet long by 11 wide. **8** Sited about 180 yards north-west of

The stoke hole at the Blind Burn still. The green remains of the circular kiln are above it **8**

the fork in the valley, it's on the north-east side of the (by now) very small burn at NT 8208 1330. In summer it's overgrown with bracken and nettles; the outline of the circular kiln at the north-west end and the stoke hole through which fuel was fed are the most obvious features. Of all the known stills in the Cheviots it is probably the most isolated.

This is a roundabout way of getting here but it's probably the easiest.

Go back the way you came, and pick up the main route at the crossing to Yearning Hall.

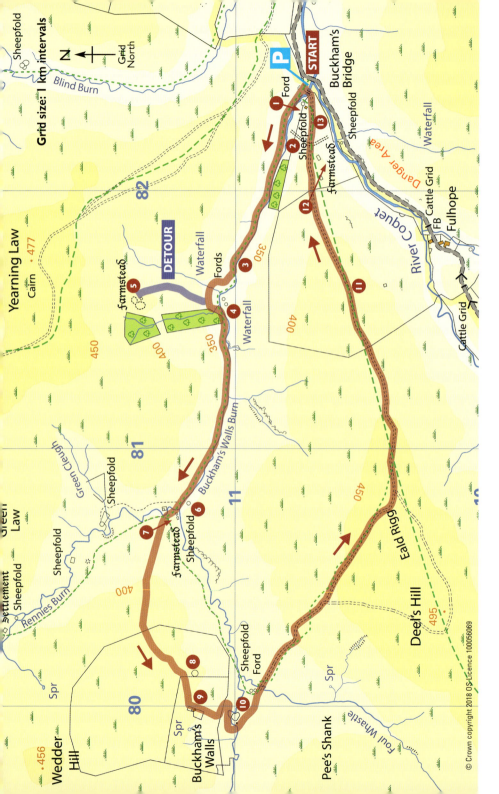

Buckham's Walls Burn and Farm

This is an area rich in the remains of ancient agriculture. It still has two working farms by the Coquet (Blindburn and Fulhope) but there are historical references to others which have either disappeared or whose names cannot be linked to existing ruins. The walk goes up the Buckham's Walls Burn, past traces of agriculture to a complex but unnamed ruin. A short climb takes you to the ruins of Buckham's Walls farm. The path passes other activity by the burn below the farm, and the circuit is completed by going over Eald Rigg, where there are yet more remains of farm buildings.

About 4 to 5 miles.   Grading: Moderate.

Park at the car park at NT 8241 1071 where the Buckham's Walls Burn joins the Coquet, about 600 yards west of Blindburn farm (NE65 7DD).

Cross the wooden bridge at the far end of the car park, go through the gate, back through a second gate on your right and climb the small hillock just beyond the stell. **①**

There is a small rectangular structure on its southern shoulder. Excavation by CCA has shown this is probably the remains of a 17th century shieling, with a hearth. Finds included remains of tobacco pipes and pottery, but there were also flint tools that may be 5000 years old, so the site has been used for a long time. From the top you can see old stock enclosures just below the hillock and also back by the car park.

Go back to the car park and follow the finger post by the information board to the track that runs along the north-east bank of the burn; head upstream.

The hillock at the start of the walk, with an old rectangular stock enclosure at its foot

Past the hillock, on the far bank, is a dyke and ditch coming down the slope – one end of a barrier enclosing a triangle of land between the Coquet and the burn. **2** This device is seen elsewhere in the Cheviots.

600 yards further on, from NT 8175 1100, you can see a mound on the far bank set at right angles to the burn. This may be the remains of a 20th-century military firing position. **3**

Cross a small stream after another 200 yards to NT 8161 1107.

The stack stand (nearest the camera) and stell by the burn. The hollow way leads down to the stream at the right **4**

On the other side of the main burn is large turf stack stand and beyond it a turf and stone stell. ④ Just upstream from them are the remains of a hollow way down to the burn, a relic of past routes up and down the valley. Heading broadly east, the path through it climbs the valley side and heads towards the abandoned farm on Eald Rigg that you will see at the end of the walk. ⑫

Detour

Turn right if you're a keen walker at around NT 8152 1108 and follow a faint path up Yearning Law.

This crosses remains of agricultural terraces or lynchets, and possibly some cord rig, but these are best visible in winter. After about 300 yards you will see a hillock, the top of which is at NT 8155 1139. ⑤

The hillock with its surrounding dyke on Yearning Law seen from above. Part of the adjacent enclosure is at bottom left ⑤

A dyke and ditch surround this hillock, forming an enclosure. On its north-east side, built over the ditch and therefore later, is a D-shaped enclosure about 90 feet across. On the south-eastern side of this at NT 8158 1139 are the remains of a three-bay building about 50 feet long, and there may be another, smaller, one on the north-west of the D at NT 8156 1141. It isn't known how old any of this is: the enclosure round the base of the hillock may be prehistoric, while the buildings might be medieval or even later.

Go back downhill to the main path.

Main Route

If you don't make this detour, you will see the hillock later (but from a distance) from Eald Rigg.

Continue along the burn for another half mile; at NT 8081 1120 you will see a sheep stell on the far bank.

This is inside a larger oval enclosure about 350 feet long and 60 wide, which is best seen by going a few yards further and a little uphill. The age of this is unknown but it must be linked to the building in the fork of Buckham's Walls Burn and Rennie's Burn less than 100 yards further on at NT 8075 1123. **7** Now a rectangular ruin, a wall with some dressed stones running across its interior suggests it has been extended, perhaps to turn an abandoned house into a sheepfold.

The ruin at the junction of the Buckham's Walls Burn with the Rennie's Burn **7**

To get to it there used to be a bridge over the Rennie's Burn, but now the best place to cross is at NT 8076 1127, a ford just 50 yards upstream to the north.

There are more enclosures to the west of the ruin, and about 80 feet away in the same direction are some old lazy beds. All this suggests the original building was a farm, but its name is not known.

Possibly connected with it are the less obvious remains of two smaller buildings about 50 yards to the north on the east bank of the Rennie's Burn at NT 8076 1128 – just by the ford.

The lazy beds to the west of the ruin **7**

Follow the left of two steep hollow ways up the hill behind the ruin; the path gradually gets fainter. Head to NT 8059 1132 where there is a slightly better track running west to a fence.

From here you can see the gable of Buckham's Wall farm ahead, to the left and slightly downhill.

Go though the gate at NT 8027 1140 and head roughly south-west to a second gate at NT 8012 1121. Before going through this, follow the fence line south for 50 yards.

Here there is a low-walled stack stand about 80 feet across. Its centre is at NT 8012 1115, and it's one of the largest in the Cheviots. **8**

Buckham's Walls farm as it is today **9**

The farm as it was circa 1930. Note the enormous peat stack to the right, east of the building. **9** Photo courtesy Bill Trobe

Return to the gate and continue for 150 yards to Buckham's Wall farm at NT 7997 1116. **9**

The main part of the ruin is a single large area with a blocked fireplace at the eastern end. Last lived in around 1940, close examination of the remains and photographs suggest it was more complex than this. The large area was divided into two; a bedroom was at the east end with the fireplace, and a kitchen and living room was to the west. A range was sited against the western wall, and there was a door through to the still-visible small extension to the north, which was probably a pantry or scullery (to the right in the picture on the previous page). The remains of wooden shelves are still visible in the walls. On the other side, another extension formed an entrance porch (on the left in the same picture); the outside door was on the eastern side of this, out of the wind. Attached to the east end of the building, towards the camera, was a byre which has almost disappeared. We don't know if the roof space was used or not, but in 1901 ten people were living here.

Head south downhill, crossing the banks of two enclosures; the more obvious one is about 40 yards below the farm. After about 100 yards bear left and follow a track across the slope to the south-east.

On the valley floor below is an irregular banked enclosure inside which are sets of ditches outlining two rectangular structures. **10** One is about 30 feet square, while the one abutting it is about half that. It isn't known know what these were for. Reach them by following the curving track

The old tedder by the burn below the farm **10**

through a gate and crossing the burn. Inside the enclosure are the rusting remains of a tedder, a horse-drawn device that turned and aerated hay. Made by Nicholson & Son of Newark, this must predate the farm's abandonment.

Head east towards a sheep stell; low linear mounds beyond it suggest the presence of earlier structures. The track passes by a brick and corrugated iron hut, crosses the stream and heads south-east onto Eald Rigg.

After about 450 yards uphill you come to a marker post at NT 8040 1063. Take the left hand fork here and continue south-east. After less than half a mile, join the track running along the top of Eald Rigg at around NT 8085 1029. Head east along the top of the ridge, passing through three gates.

After the second gate, at around NT 8156 1052 and just over half a mile to the north, you'll see the site on the flank of Yearning Law described in the earlier detour. **5** The most obvious part of it is the well-defined hillock about halfway up the slope. The dyke around its base can be seen as can the green area to the right with the enclosure and possible farmstead.

At NT 8161 1048, about 30 yards south of track, is the old TV aerial that once served the farm at Fulhope in the valley below. **11** Future archaeologists may well wonder what this was.

Turn right just past the third gate to an area of disturbed ground starting close to the path that covers about an acre. **12**

The probable remains of the farmhouse on Eald Rigg **12**

This was once another farm, but we know nothing of its history. A low-walled enclosure about 20 feet wide and 45 feet long lies across the slope at NT 8207 1066, with a deep ditch outside the north wall. A similar structure has been built at right-angles to this at NT 8206 1060. This is 50 feet long and 18 wide, with an entrance at the south end and some stone in the eastern wall. Banks to its east could be lazy beds, or possibly what's left of earlier enclosures. At the south-east corner of the area, at NT 8213 1066, are the remains of what may have been a small farmhouse, about 33 feet long and 14 wide. There are remains of stone walls with a few finished faces, but there is now no obvious entrance. Its eastern end abuts a small enclosure.

A bank encircles the whole area around the farmstead; this is now best seen near the path at around NT 8211 1068.

Return to the path; about 200 yards beyond the third gate, at NT 8219 1069, it crosses the dyke mentioned earlier in the walk that lies between the Coquet and the Buckham's Walls Burn. ❷

Another low dyke runs parallel with the path about 100 yards past this and 50 feet down the hill at NT 8228 1066. This is the north bank of an enclosure about 60 feet wide; dykes on its other edges run for the same distance down the hill, where there is a rectangular structure about 50 feet long and 20 wide. ⓭   It's now in a wet area, so it may have been a byre rather than a house, but the steep slope of the enclosure above it is not ideal for stock. There are other dykes nearby; one is immediately to the east of the enclosure and another is on lower ground 60 yards further east again. We have no history for these remains and they have never been excavated. It's possible they are linked to the farmstead 200 yards back up the path.

Given that they are both on Eald Rigg, they may have a connection with a 17th-century reference to a farm called *Elrigburn*.

Return to the car park about 100 yards further on.

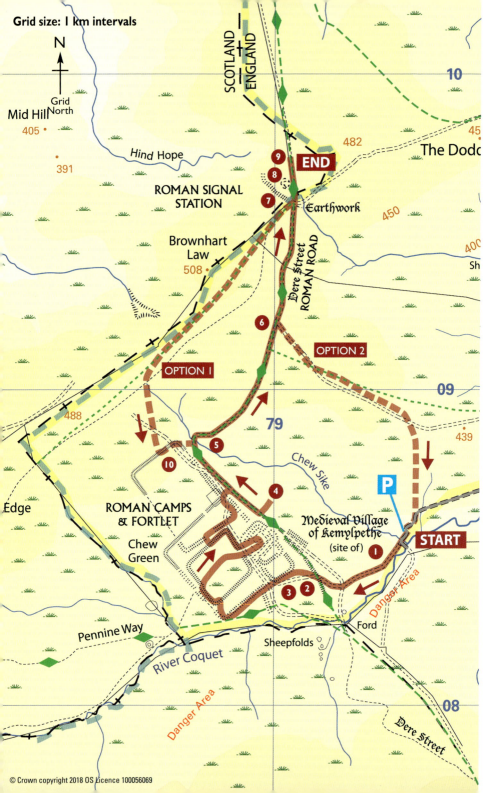

Dere Street, Chew Green and the Border

Dere Street was the Roman road that linked York with Hadrian's Wall and points north. The camp at Chew Green was one of a series along the road between the fort at Bremenium (Rochester) and the Antonine Wall. Parts of it may have been built by Agricola *circa* AD 80, but it is unclear how much or when it was used thereafter.

The first part of the walk consists of a tour round the camp. It is sometimes hard to work out what is going on here, and a plan of the camp helps you understand the bigger picture. Not all the earthworks are Roman; some are medieval and there are also the remains of a medieval settlement.

You can turn back after seeing the camp, but the full walk goes up to the Border, passing a ruined farm and visiting what may be the site of a Roman signal station. You can then either come back by the same route, go over Brownhart Law, or follow a path across the moors back to the car park.

Distance: about 3½ or 4 miles in total depending on the return route.

Grading: Moderate.

Use the Chew Green parking area at NT 794 085. This is nearly two miles past Fulhope (NE65 7BX), the last working farm in the valley. Follow the road downhill for 40 yards to a gate ahead and go up the track beyond.

There is a small enclosure on the right which can be seen ahead of you as you go down the road. ❶ It's not clear what this was for; it would have been awkward to manage stock on such a steep slope.

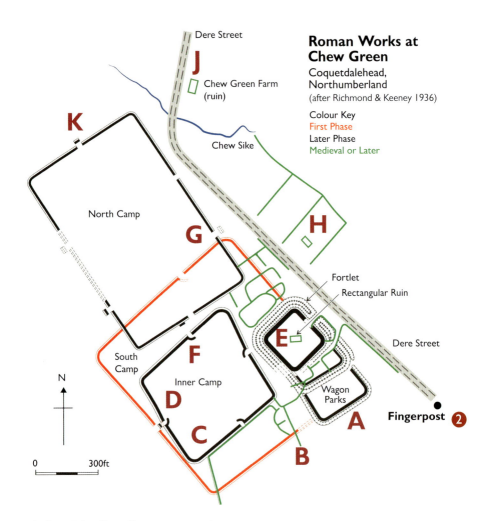

A plan of the Chew Green camps and structures

It is thought the South Camp was the first structure at Chew Green, perhaps built circa AD 80. Other Roman camps, the fortlet and the wagon parks followed. The Inner Camp may not have been for troops, but rather workers who maintained Dere Street. For more details see Chapter 8 in The Old Tracks through the Cheviots.

Continue for 300 yards to NT 7922 0832, where there's a fingerpost on a track coming up the slope from the south-east. ❷

This is Dere Street, and it runs alongside the camps. The walk does not follow it at this stage, but zigzags across the camps to give you an idea of their shape and the scale that survives after 2000 years.

Look uphill and you will see a bank parallel with the far side of the path. Cross this and about 100 yards away is a dyke running across the slope above you. Walk to it at **3** and (**A**) on the Chew Green plan on the facing page (NT 7905 0841).

You are on the downhill side of an enclosure surrounded by a dyke with a deep ditch. There are more dykes further uphill. Throughout the walk, we refer to the defences of the camps themselves as ramparts. Other banks, which may be medieval or Roman, are called dykes.

The enclosure here is too small to be a normal Roman camp. Richmond and Keeney investigated the area in the 1930s and they thought it was a part of a set of Roman wagon parks where transport convoys could park safely near troops. These might have been carrying goods like food. We know that the Roman army imported items such as figs, lentils and durum wheat for their soldiers.

The medieval boundary dyke running down the slope (**B**)

Look across the valley to the hillside to the south. Erosion from millennia of traffic has created ridges and mounds all over the slope. Dere Street is probably the diagonal line two-thirds of the way up the hill that drops from left to right before turning in a zig-zag.

Walk to (**B**), about 120 yards to the south-west at NT 7896 0836.

Here there are medieval enclosures up the hill and what is probably a medieval boundary dyke running downhill below you. The bank ahead and running south-west is the rampart of the Roman South Camp whose south-eastern part has been destroyed by later building.

Continue south-west for 170 yards along this rampart to where a ditch and dyke cut through the south-west corner of the camp at NT 7884 0827. Walk up the dyke to NT 7884 0832. (**C**)

A prominent rampart runs across the slope. This is the southern defence of a later camp built inside the first. The ditch running downhill may have been built to drain the rampart ditch, although Richmond and Keeney thought it was medieval.

Head south-west along the rampart of this later Inner Camp and then follow it as it turns north-west. 80 yards after this is an opening at NT 7875 0837. (**D**)

The junction of the Inner Camp rampart and the drainage ditch (**C**)

Here a causeway across the main ditch allows entry to the Inner Camp. The eroded rampart of the older South Camp can be seen ten yards away to the west. A gap in the main rampart acted as a 'gate' into the Inner Camp. These were just openings, but were sometimes protected by other earthworks.

The prominent eastern rampart ditch of the Inner Camp. The eroded tracks down the slope to the south mentioned on page 87 can be seen on the left in the distance

Head approximately north-east from this gate along a faint path across the camp. After 180 yards you'll come to the opposite rampart and gate. Here again a causeway crosses the very prominent ditch. Once over this, cross three parallel ramparts until you are at NT 7893 0851 inside the Roman fortlet. (**E**)

The triple ramparts at the fortlet (**E**)

The triple rampart does not go right round the fortlet, perhaps because bedrock got in the way. Richmond and Keeney suggested this was a command post, and one of the later structures on the site, and they thought they had found an earlier one underneath it. The outline of a rectangular building can be seen in the centre. This was excavated in the 1880s by a man called Clement Hodges; he later suggested it was a medieval chapel, but although widely repeated the evidence for this is very tenuous.

More of the wagon park enclosures are visible down the hill from the fortlet. From its north-eastern side look north towards the gentle incline of Brownhart Law. Multiple lines running from left to right across the far slope show generations of tracks based on Dere Street. Below these, nearer and slightly to the right, are low banks marking old field boundaries on the far side of Chew Sike. Some of these may be medieval and linked to the settlement on the near side of the sike.

Go back the way you came over the triple rampart to the single rampart of the Inner Camp. Follow this north-west for 80 yards and then continue for another 60 yards as it turns south-west, crossing two small (modern) gaps in it before coming to the north gate of the Inner Camp at NT 7880 0851. (**F**)

Looking north from this gate are yet more ramparts. 25 yards away is the southern rampart of a third camp – the North Camp – and 75 yards away is the north rampart of the South Camp – the first camp you came to on this walk. Just on the near side of the ditch in front of the closer rampart is a faint low bank about 15 feet long. This may be the remains of a *titulus* protecting the north gate of the Inner Camp; this was an external earthwork built to discourage direct attack.

Walk for about 120 yards to the north-east along the southern rampart of the North Camp, which is lower than the rampart of the Inner Camp on your right. Also on your right, after the Inner Camp rampart turns away, you pass banks defining medieval enclosures; follow the rampart of the North Camp as it turns north-west and walk for 70 yards to NT 7883 0865.

This is the intersection of the ramparts of the overlapping North and South Camps. (**G**) The north rampart of the South Camp comes in from the south-west and can be seen curving round to the south-east. There is some general damage but the eastern rampart of the North Camp has clearly been built over the South Camp rampart, so must be later.

Walk about ten yards east to the Dere Street path, turn right and follow it south-east towards the fortlet. After 60 yards you come to a small bridge (the first one) of three paving stones at NT 7888 0862; a low dyke heads off to the left at right angles. Walk 15 yards along this and then turn right for ten yards to NT 7889 0863. (**H**) on plan and **4** on map.

First recorded in the 13th century, the medieval settlement or village of Kemylpeth was probably in this area. There are several low banks around here that mark old enclosures or yards, and there's a hollow way about 30 yards further east. However, the small rectangular outline here, about 18 feet by six, seems to be the only surviving indication of a building.

Return to Dere Street. At this point, it's easy to go back to the car by going south-east to the fingerpost you first encountered; otherwise turn right and head north-west along the track.

After 200 yards, at NT 7876 0875, there are two large hollows on the right that may be the remains of quarrying. A little further on, with the rampart of the North Camp on your left, the track turns half right down to a bridge over Chew Sike. Just after this turn, look across

The remains of the Chew Green farmhouse

the sike and a bit downstream where the remains of Chew Green farmhouse can be seen on the far bank; the site is often distinctly greener than the surrounding area.

Cross the bridge and 12 stones before the top of the steps take a small track to the right; cross a hollow way then after 35 yards you reach the farmhouse at NT 7878 0882. (J) on plan and ❺ on map.

Probably abandoned in the late 18th century, the main building consists of two rooms; other earthworks and mounds nearby may be the remains of a byre, or else a midden – a domestic rubbish dump. Tracks on either side of the farm are the signs of old routes across the sike and up the hill. Writing around 1900, David Dippie Dixon reported old drinking glasses and tobacco pipes being found here. He suggested it was the site of an old inn, but it was probably just a farm that catered for passing travellers.

Return to the track and continue north-east on Dere Street, past a fingerpost at NT 7901 0922. ❻

At NT 7902 0930 you will see a fence and a gate ahead, with the slightly convex outline of the Roman Dere Street *agger* visible against the skyline. With generations of tracks across the hillside the actual route of the Roman road is often hard to trace, but this is a good view of it.

Feral goats on the cross dyke west of Dere Street ❼

Go through the gate and then another at the top of the slope at NT 7907 0961; then use the gate in the fence on your left. Turn south back along the fence for about 35 yards to NT 7904 0959.

A heather-covered dyke, with a ditch on either side, heads north-west for over 100 yards with the final section dropping down a steep slope. **7** This is the western section of a cross dyke, the central portion of which was destroyed by Dere Street and later peat cutting. The surviving eastern section starts at NT 7909 0956 and runs south-east for about 130 yards.

Return to the gate, but don't go through it. Follow the fence north for 20 yards.

You are now on the eastern side of an earthwork that forms a roughly circular structure up to 80 feet across, the centre of which is at NT 7904 0964. **8** Towards the west the earthwork splits into two banks and two or three ditches.

This is commonly believed to be the site of a Roman signal station – and it may have been one – although a small dig in 1946 found no proof of this. It has good views to the west, with Rubers Law about 13 miles away. But any signalling system must have been very simple, and would have been impractical in cloud or mist. What's more, the site cannot

Rubers Law from the 'signal station' **8**

The quarries next to Dere Street **9**

even be seen from Chew Green, whereas a signal station on the top of Thirl Moor, about a mile to the south, could have been seen from both Chew Green and the Roman fort at Bremenium (Rochester) further south.

Return to Dere Street and go north for nearly 200 yards to NT 7904 0977.

There are two adjacent pits on the west side of the fence. **9** These are the remains of quarries which would have been used for material to make and maintain the road. There are smaller pits at several places further along the route, and a large set about a mile away next to a stretch of Dere Street that it still very boggy.

This is the end of the walk. You can either go back by the same route or take one of two other options (the dashed lines on the map).

Option 1

This uses the 'Alternative Pennine Way' path marked on the fingerpost by the gate you went through at the top of the uphill stretch from Chew Green at NT 7907 0961.

Follow the path across Brownhart Law to around NT 7842 0906 and then head south down to the northern rampart of the North Camp, aiming for NT 7861 0878. There is no real path on this stretch but it's only about 300 yards and the going is fairly easy.

You will arrive at **10** on the map and (**K**) on the plan – the north gate of the North Camp; this has a recognisable *titulus* some eight to ten yards outside it.

Turn left along the rampart back towards Dere Street, where you turn right and return the way you first came, past the fortlet and back to the car park.

Option 2

Go back past the 'Alternative Pennine Way' fingerpost and head downhill until you reach the fingerpost at NT 7901 0922. **6** Turn left, following the track signed Makendon.

After a bit this track starts to curve left and at NT 7924 0900 follow a path that bears slightly off to the right. At NT 7953 0876 you will see the car park on your right and a track heading downhill towards the road.

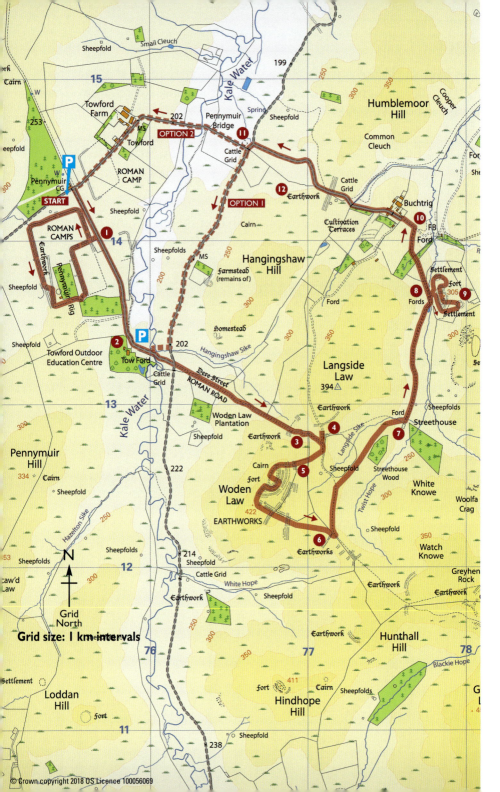

Dere Street: Pennymuir, Woden Law and Moat Knowe

This walk focuses on three outstanding sites around a stretch of Dere Street in the Scottish Cheviots – the Pennymuir Roman camps, the Iron Age structures on Woden Law and the Dark Age fort of Moat Knowe.

Getting to the top of Woden Law involves a climb of 700 feet, but on a good day the views are more than worth it.

Distance: About 8 miles; optionally less if you return after Woden Law.

Grading: Moderate.

Park at the south-west corner of the Pennymuir crossroads at NT 7549 1430. About ten miles south-east of Jedburgh, the postcode for the area is TD8 6NH.

There is an information board here about the two Roman camps to the south. It's helpful, but it says there are only traces of a later camp, although you will see the remains are actually quite prominent. It also describes a layout for the camp's interior; this is rather speculative and at the very least it overestimates the relative sizes of accommodation for senior units and lower ranks.

The building on the other side of the road stands on the site of an old inn. The land behind it was used for large agricultural fairs and shows.

Walk downhill along the road to the south (Dere Street) for 450 yards to NT 7571 1395, passing a stile and fingerpost on your right. **❶**

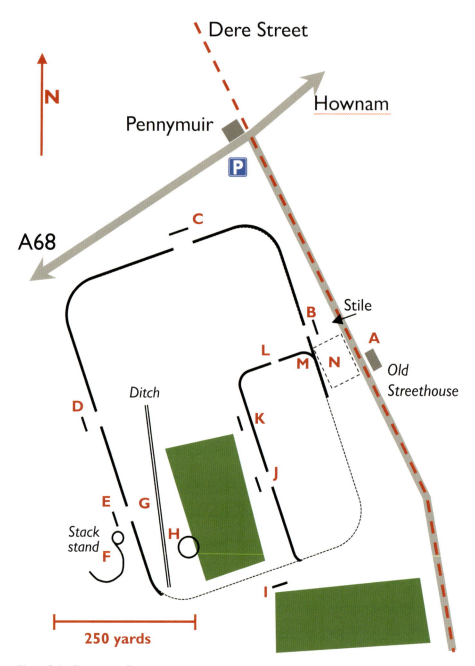

N

Dere Street

Hownam

Pennymuir

P

A68

C

Stile

B

A

L

M

N

Old
Streethouse

Ditch

K

D

J

E

G

H

Stack
stand

F

I

250 yards

Plan of the Pennymuir Roman camps

Just over the fence on your left (the east), is a rectangular platform about 60 feet long and 25 wide. See (**A**) on the plan of the Pennymuir camps. A farm called Streethouse once stood here. Shown on a map of around 1750 by William Roy, a cartographer who supported the English Army in Scotland, it has disappeared but the name was re-used elsewhere. South of it, banks form an enclosure about 90 yards long and 40 wide. Over the road another bank runs up the slope; this is the southern boundary of a second enclosure or field 80 yards long and 45 wide, almost certainly part of the Streethouse farm. (**N** on plan).

Walk back up the road for about 80 yards to the stile and fingerpost at NT 7567 1402. These are now on your left; cross the stile.

On your left is the bank that defines the northern edge of the field just described, so it's not Roman.

Walk away from the road, parallel with this bank, for 40 yards.

Another bank lies across your path. (**B**) About 50 feet long, it's a Roman *titulus* – an earthwork that defended an opening or gate through a rampart into a camp. The rampart in question is about ten yards further up the slope and is best seen as it heads off north (to your right). This is the eastern rampart of the earlier, bigger camp on the site. Slightly further away, up the hill and on the left, a larger rampart runs down the slope. This is the northern defence of the second, later camp.

Head north along the first rampart. The gaps in it are not original and it gets more eroded as you proceed. After 240 yards you reach the north-east corner of the camp at NT 7554 1419; turn left (west) along the well-defined north rampart, avoiding the gorse there.

The next gap you reach, after 45 yards, is modern, but after another 100 yards, before you reach a ruined sheep stell, you come to the camp's north gate at NT 7541 1416. (**C**) Again, this is protected by a *titulus* some 15 yards north of the gate. Like the first one this is also about 50 feet long, which seems to be the standard size for this camp.

Continue for another 200 yards to the camp's north-west corner and then turn left and head south along the western rampart.

As you walk along it, look around to get a feel for how large this camp is: it covers over 40 acres. This rampart has two gates in it. The first,

*The titulus at the north gate of the main camp. (**C**) on plan*

after 220 yards, is at NT 7528 1389 (**D**) and the second, 170 yards further on, is at NT 7534 1374. (**E**) Both are protected by *tituli*.

Pause at the second gate; walk about 12 yards south from its *titulus*.

At NT 7531 1370 is a low circular earthwork about 45 feet in diameter; with no obvious entrance it is probably a post-medieval stack stand. Attached to it and stretching away further to the south is a long, curved earthwork that presumably fulfilled some stock management function. (**F**) Both these structures were shown on Roy's 18th-century map.

Return to the gate in the rampart and then head east for 40 yards, reaching a broad ditch at NT 7538 1374. (**G**)

This is marked on the OS map as medieval, although it's not clear what evidence there is for this. Set at an angle to the Roman rampart, it gets very shallow as it heads north but with care it can be traced almost as far as the northern rampart. There are records of it once being visible beyond the metalled road. Its function is unknown.

Turn right and head south along the side of this ditch for about 75 yards. Turn left at NT 7535 1367.

After 45 yards you come to a large circular enclosure, just over 100 feet across and centred on NT 7541 1368. (**H**) With its east side in the trees, this was almost certainly for stock. Like the stack stand and the curved bank you've just seen, it was also shown on Roy's map.

Return to the ditch and walk south for some 80 yards until it disappears.

Here you are only 40 feet from the western rampart, which also disappears at NT 7539 1359 – the south-west corner of the camp. The southern rampart has disappeared completely, presumably destroyed by farming and, especially further east, by erosion.

Head slightly north of east towards the gap in the trees. After 200 yards, at NT 7555 1365 go through a gap in the fence, and then immediately turn right along it for about 35 yards.

Here you will find a solitary *titulus* at NT 7555 1362. (**I**) Although the southern rampart has vanished, this was just outside the place where the camp's south gate must have been.

Return to where you left the gap in the fence and walk east for 60 yards. At this point (NT 7558 1367) you come to the southern end of the western rampart of the second camp. Turn left (north) and walk along it.

After 130 yards, at NT 7554 1378, is one of the two gates in this rampart. (**J**) It's protected by a *titulus*, but this one is only 30 feet long. 110 yards further on at NT 7551 1387 is a second, similarly-sized *titulus*. (**K**) However, this one is not opposite any discernible gap in the ramparts. Was it built in anticipation of a gate? Or was the gate filled in?

Continue for another 80 yards to the north-west corner of this, the second camp, and then turn right along the northern rampart. After 60 yards you pass the north gate (NT 7556 1396), (**L**) and another 60 yards brings you to the north-east corner of the camp at NT 7563 1397. (**M**)

The western rampart of the smaller camp near (J)

This is the area you saw from the first *titulus* you encountered after leaving the road. The eastern rampart of the first camp can be seen coming down from the north on your left, and the rampart of the second camp you are following clearly overlies it as it turns right and south along the same line. The rampart's ditch is prominent here, but the structures disappear after 80 yards to the south, destroyed by old ploughing.

The banks in the area between this stretch of rampart and the road are those that define the field or enclosure you saw earlier.

Return to the road. Optionally, take the car and drive south past the camps. Park at NT 7599 1332 before crossing Kale Water; this will make your walk a bit shorter – especially if you don't do the full second part of it. If you don't do this, turn right on the road and walk down the hill to Kale Water.

On your way you pass the old Towford school up among trees on your right. ❷ on map. This closed in 1964 and is now an outdoor centre.

Cross the bridge over Kale Water and head up to the T-junction. Use the stile on the other side of the road and go south-east up the track beyond, signposted Dere Street.

The raised area of ground along which the track runs may well be the remains of the *agger*, the convex centre of a Roman road.

Cross a stile by a gate in the wall on your right after 130 yards and continue uphill through a small valley for just over half a mile.

About three-quarters of the way up, at NT 7687 1284 and about 20 yards before the fence on your left changes direction slightly, if the vegetation is low you will see a short length of a substantial dyke up the slope on your right. ❸ In its original form it probably predated Dere Street which has contributed to the disappearance of its central section. There is no sign of it immediately on the left of the path, but a short stretch of it can be seen on the other side of the valley.

As you reach the top, turn left to a small block-shaped building at NT 7709 1278. ❹ Now surrounded by sheep folds this was once a dwelling called Streethouse. It may have taken its name from the farm opposite the Roman camps when that was abandoned; this one was last lived in

Streethouse, with the adjacent pens and field **4**

during the 1860s. The sides facing the prevailing winds and weather have no doors or windows and the high walls protect the sloping roof.

Return to where you arrived at the top of the climb, opposite the southernmost gates of the sheepfolds around Streethouse. Take the grassy path ahead and slightly to the right that continues up Woden Law to the Iron Age camp on its summit. Follow it for 130 yards until you reach a gate at NT 7701 1264.

Go through this and head for a second gate further on, just to the left of the fence running up the hill on your right. 40 yards short of the gate you cross a single dyke at NT 7692 1263. **5** on map and (**P**) on the Woden Law plan overleaf. Go past this and through the gate.

Immediately after this is a second, more complex set of earthworks at NT 7687 1262, with multiple parallel dykes and corresponding ditches. (**Q**) You will see the southern part of these – and that of the first one – later, but the relationship of these external dykes with the ramparts of the camp, which are further uphill, is not clear. Two archaeologists, Richmond and Keeney, investigated Woden Law in the 1950s and suggested that they were Roman, built for siege practice after the camp had been conquered. Although a plausible suggestion, most archaeologists now believe that these dykes also date from the Iron Age.

Continue uphill for another 50 yards to the ramparts round the camp on the top of the hill at NT 7683 1260. (**R**)

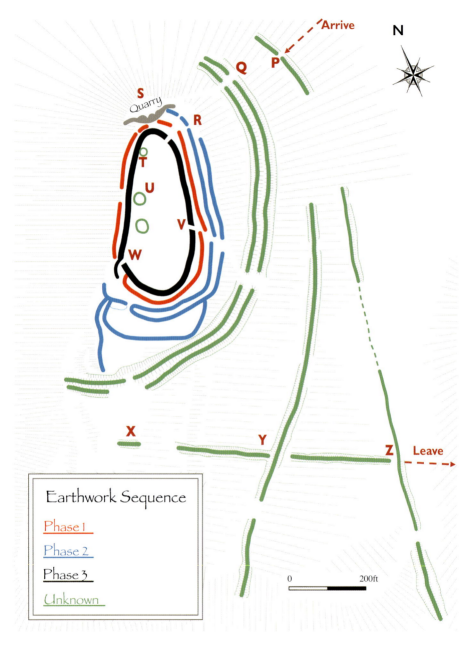

Plan of the structures on Woden Law

*Part of the external dykes at Woden Law. (**Q**) on plan*

Again, these are complex. Starting from the lowest point, there is a pair of ramparts and ditches, then another rampart and finally a slope leading to a fourth rampart at the top. Richmond and Keeney suggested that the third rampart was the earliest, and that the two below it were built later, in anticipation of a Roman attack. In their opinion, excavations in the ditches here showed that the pair had been abandoned soon after construction, and that the innermost rampart, the one at the top of the slope, was the latest, built when the camp was subsequently reoccupied.

Turn right (north-west) just below the ramparts and walk round to the northern end of the hill.

A large exposed rock face is almost certainly the remains of a quarry, the source of the stone used in many of the ramparts. (**S**)

Retrace your steps to the path and enter the camp itself. Walk across it to the western side. (**T**)

You are at the top of a steep slope dropping away to Kale Water. On a clear day there are extensive views to the north and west; the three peaks of the Eildon Hills overlooking the Roman site of Trimontium are clearly visible. The innermost rampart goes all the way round the camp, but here on the west there are fewer traces of other fortifications below

*The quarry at the north end of Woden Law (**S**)*

it. They have either collapsed down the slope or else were not originally built, with the slope providing a natural defence.

Two hollows here at NT 7679 1259 may once have held small buildings or shelters immediately next to the rampart.

Turn left and walk south along the rampart for 25 yards.

On your left at NT 7677 1256 are the faint traces of a roundhouse 35 feet across. (**U**) This is one of the few signs of dwellings inside the camp.

Turn left 20 yards after this at a point where the path drops into a slight hollow. Walk east across the camp.

At NT 7678 1251 a vertical standing stone – an orthostat – marks one side of one of the original entrances to the camp. (**V**)

*The view from the western rampart (**T**) with the two hollows in the foreground*

*The eastern entrance (**V**)*

Turn right and follow the rampart south to the southern end of the camp.

This is a confused area, full of ramparts, hollows and enclosures. Called an annexe, it's formed by the more complex set of external dykes you passed earlier turning to the west and wrapping themselves around the end of the camp's ramparts, which have also been extended.

Follow the inner rampart as it curves round to the west and back towards the slope down to Kale Water.

At the top of the slope, at NT 7674 1253, is another of the original entrances to the camp, with more orthostats. (**W**)

Leave the camp by the track through this entrance and follow it south through the annexe, eventually crossing the last major dyke at NT 7671 1244. 60 yards beyond this, at NT 7668 1239, turn left (east) next to a short, low fragment of another dyke. (**X**) After a gap it reappears as you follow a faint path in the same direction and approach the fence posts marking the corner of a field.

This dyke continues down the slope, and was built almost at right angles to the other external dykes you crossed before entering the camp itself.

Indeed, as you follow it downhill you will cross the extension of one of them, as well as an additional one. The intersection with the latter is

*The south-western entrance (**W**)*

the first at NT 7678 1234. (**Y**) More obvious on the left than the right, it is wide, about 20 feet across between the adjacent ditches and can be traced for 200 yards to the left, and half that to the right.

At the foot of the slope, at NT 7687 1230, you cross the second dyke. (**Z**) This one is more obvious on the right than the left. Some 400 yards long, it lines up with the very first dyke you crossed on the climb up Woden Law. The dyke you have been following stops in this area.

Continue on the same line up the slope in front of you. There is no

*The broad dyke at (**Y**)*

path, but once over the top and descending again, aim towards a sheep stell low on the other side of the valley ahead. On reaching a fence turn right to NT 7714 1221, and the ruined end of a cross dyke. **6** on map.

This can be traced for about 120 yards along the hillside to the south-west. There is a gap in it here because a section of it was destroyed by Dere Street, which is the track on the other side of the fence. A short length can be seen on the other side of the Roman road.

Follow the fence south-east for 130 yards to NT 7722 1211; go through the gate there, turn left, and follow Dere Street back to the north-west. 50 yards after re-passing the cross dyke on your left, stop and look back.

You can see the other section of the dyke on the eastern side of Dere Street, dropping down towards the valley floor. Like other such dykes, the damage done by the Roman road is a strong suggestion that it was built earlier. It may have acted as a boundary marker or a line of defence along a prehistoric route that predated Dere Street.

Follow the track, which turns north after a slight curve. The stone wall on the south side of the field next to Streethouse comes into view, and soon after this follow a path that forks off to the right (north-east) at NT 7716 1242. This approaches the wall, meeting it at the eastern corner of the field; go through the gate there at NT 7730 1266. Continue on the track, roughly parallel with a plantation on your right. The track gets fainter after the trees, but continue north-east, aiming for a sheep stell on the far slope.

As the path approaches the valley floor it passes a pile of debris on the right at NT 7758 1284. This is the remains of a building here, also called Streethouse, that is still marked on some maps. **7** At the foot of the slope the track becomes clearer as it curves left and heads north over a sike at NT 7761 1290.

Continue on the track for 600 yards; the conical hill ahead is your next destination, the Dark Age fort of Moat Knowe. Pass a pond on your right at NT 7775 1356 and 60 yards further on cross a stile over the fence on your right that runs along the base of the hill. **8** Turn right again (south) on a path just the other side of it and follow it as it curves uphill and round the southern end of Moat Knowe.

At the top of the slope you will see a large circular enclosure ahead, between you and the fence on the near skyline. **9** on map and (**a**) on the Moat Knowe picture. 50 yards across, with an entrance on the south side, there are substantial stones in its walls. Inside are some raised areas but there are no signs of dwellings. It's impossible to date without excavation and its use is uncertain, but its substantial construction suggests some importance.

*Stones in the bank of the enclosure below Moat Knowe (**a**)*

Retrace your steps along the south-eastern flank of Moat Knowe. At its southern tip, before descending the slope you came up, take a track to the right that curves round as it goes up the hill.

A structure called a nuclear fort, Moat Knowe is unusual. Excavations at similar sites elsewhere in Scotland suggest it may date from the 7th or 8th centuries. The fort has a central nucleus (hence 'nuclear'), surrounded on either side by courtyards; in the case of Moat Knowe there are four of these, two on each side at successively lower levels.

Just after the curve in the track you come to the west side of the first of these yards. (**b**) It is defined by banks on the east and south and by the natural slope of the hill on the north. On the west, however, a set of vertically-set stones (orthostats) separates it from the track running past. Some of these have fallen, but others remain upright. There are more orthostats on the other side of the track, along its edge above the steep slope.

Moat Knowe showing key features in the text

Continue along the track.

Immediately up the hill is the second of the two southern courtyards. (**c**) Like the first, and the other two you'll pass later, it contains no real signs of buildings or dwellings, although there are one or two flattish areas.

Next you come to the nucleus (**d**), built around the top of the narrow ridge-shaped hill with a series of terraces rising from the track towards the summit to the east. These are probably natural in origin, but may well have been enhanced by quarrying for stone to use elsewhere in the fort.

Orthostats at the southern courtyard
*(**b**) and along the track*

*The bank defining the eastern edges of the two northern courtyards (**e**, **f**)*

Climb to the top: the imposing hill to the north is Hownam Law.

Return to the track, turn right and continue north. The track disappears briefly, but a narrow path follows a ridge that descends past the other two courtyards. (**e** and **f**)

The track reappears as the path curves round the north end of the hill, just after you cross a prominent bank that runs down the spine of the hill and defines the eastern edges of the two northern courtyards.

Follow the track down to the base of the hill, and then turn back to the left and north again.

At NT 7789 1375, 30 yards south-east of a more overgrown area, is a circular structure formed by low banks. (**g**) About 40 feet across, it's hard to identify an entrance, but there may have been one on the north side. Like the larger circular enclosure, it's undateable. It could be a much-decayed stack stand for fodder, or it may have served some protective purpose for people or small numbers of stock.

Head west over a jumbled line of boulders towards the northern end of the main hill.

On a large platform just to the north of it, and centred on NT 7781 1376, is a set of crude, irregularly-shaped enclosures. These have also been eroded, but some entrances are still visible, as are the remains of

*The building remains at the northern end of Moat Knowe (**h**)*

one or two buildings. (**h**) Based on their shapes, the development is believed to be medieval, and it's possible that the small circular structure was in some way linked with it.

Follow a path south (**i**) along the western side of Moat Knowe, with a steep drop to the burn on your right. This leads to the stile which you used to enter the site. Cross this, return to the broad track beyond, turn right and head north for 100 yards to a gate at NT 7773 1373. Keep going for another 400 yards, through some trees to a T-junction with another farm track at NT 7766 1406. ⑩ on map.

Turn left here and follow the track uphill, past a cottage and the farm at Buchtrig. It then becomes a metalled road which, after an initial descent and ascent, continues downhill into the Kale Water valley. 1100 yards after Buchtrig you reach a T-junction at NT 7665 1458. ⑪

Look to your left as you drop into the valley. In the right conditions you will see agricultural terracing on the slopes of the fields there, suggesting that they were once all under cultivation. ⑫

Turn left at the T-junction. If your car is at Kale Water go straight ahead for about a mile. If it's at the Pennymuir crossroads turn right after 50 yards. Follow the road uphill; it swings left at Towford farm and Pennymuir is straight ahead. This is also about a mile.

Glossary

Agger	the slightly domed centre of a Roman road.
Agricultural Terracing	terraces built on a hillside to make cultivation easier.
Bronze Age	a period from around 2200 BC to 750 BC when bronze was the main metal in use.
Byre	a building, or part of one, used to house stock.
Cord Rig	an early form of rig and furrow that is close-set and created by hand ploughing.
Cross Dyke	a dyke built across a ridge, but whose precise purpose is unknown.
Dark Ages	see Early Medieval.
Droving	the movement of stock over long distances for commercial reasons.
Dyke	a usually earthen bank, often with an adjacent ditch. Used for defence or to mark a boundary.
Fulling	a process for tightening up and removing grease from newly-woven cloth.
Haugh	an area of low flat land next to a watercourse.
Head Dyke	a dyke separating arable land from moorland.
Hollow Ways	deeply eroded tracks formed by heavy traffic.
Iron Age	a period from around 750 BC to the arrival of the Romans in AD 43.
Iron Age Camps	also hillforts. Iron Age structures often covering an acre or more and enclosed by ramparts.
Kiln	a chamber for drying (e.g. barley) or burning (e.g. lime).
Lazy Beds	small-scale hand-crafted rig and furrow, usually for horticulture not agriculture.
Longhouse	a medieval or post-medieval rectangular building that housed both people and stock.
Lynchets	cultivation terraces that run across a slope. Perhaps built with a hand plough called an ard.
Malting	part of the whisky-making process, where barley is spread out, and damped so it germinates. It is then kiln-dried.
Marching Camps	temporary camps, used by Roman troops in transit.

Medieval	a period also called the Middle Ages.
Early	from the fall of the Roman empire to the end of the first millennium. Also called the Dark Ages.
High	from the first millennium to *circa* AD 1300.
Late	from *circa* AD 1300 to *circa* AD 1500.
Mesolithic	in the British Isles, a period from around 8000 BC to 4000 BC.
Neolithic	in the British Isles, a period from the introduction of farming in around 4000 BC to 2200 BC.
Nuclear Fort	a defensive site from the Dark Ages with courtyards around a central nucleus.
Orthostat	a large stone set vertically on an edge, often part of a wall.
Palisade	a wooden wall built for defence. Two concentric ones formed a double palisade.
Pele	a defensive tower usually built by high-status individuals and dating from the 14th to the 16th centuries.
Post-medieval	a period from the 16th century onward.
Reivers	raiders involved in cattle theft and other illegal activities.
Rig and Furrow	sets of ridges and furrows produced by ploughing a field in a regular pattern.
Romano-British	used to describe native British activities during the period of Roman occupation.
Roundhouse	an early form of circular house, built from wood and perhaps stone with a conical roof.
Scooped Settlement	a settlement on a platform dug back into a slope.
Sheep Stell	a circular structure used for sheep management and shelter.
Shieling	a poorly-built dwelling typically used during transhumance.
Sike	a small stream, often in marshy ground.
Stack Stand	a place where fodder could be stored and protected from stock.
Steading	a farm and its buildings.
Still	a site or building used for the production of spirits.
Titulus	a bank outside a gate of a Roman camp, built to protect the opening from direct attack.
Tobacco Pipes	small clay smoking pipes used from the early 17th century.
Transhumance	the movement of stock to the uplands for summer grazing.

Notes

Notes

Notes